OFFICIAL CONTACT

THE END OF EARTH ISOLATION

RODRIGO FREITAS

CONECTAR

Official Contact: The End of Earth Isolation

Copyright © 2019 by Rodrigo Freitas

ISBN: 978-85-62411-51-9

1st Edition 2019, San Francisco - CA

Conectar Publisher

Publisher: Gabriela de Paula Pessoa Freitas

Coordenation: Krysamon Cavalcante

www.conectareditora.com.br

CONTENTS

FOREWORD

My name is Rogério, better known as Jan Val Ellam, which is the pseudonym I chose when I had to publish my first book "Cosmic Reintegration", back in 1996 to try to preserve my image.

Today, more than twenty years later, having published more than 35 books, having done an uncountable number of lectures, I realize that it was in vain. It was impossible for me to keep myself in the shadows as one day I intended to.

Rodrigo Freitas, the author of this book, is my son and this book is inspired by my work. When I published my first book he was only fourteen years old and I tried never to influence him (or anybody else) to read my books, but he did. When he was about sixteen, he started reading the books I had published and started to find out what I was involved with. It was a slow process...

It took us until about 2010 to better understand the process that involved us, to understand that this universe indeed has a creator and that this creator was behind part of the phenomena that was happening to me.

As I use to say, my life was transformed into an alien desk, and also into a spiritual desk. These beings kept on saying that I had to publish all these books because otherwise no one would, and when I realized the importance of such content I struggled and with many difficulties and help from third parties, I was able to transmit all this in the way I could, the way it was possible.

Rodrigo has always tried to help me with this task, and now, because he speaks better English than I do, he is helping me to bring all this information to English. This book and some videos that we are producing are only the first steps.

We are about to see many spaceships in our skies, we are about to see the first official contact with beings from other worlds and dimensions and we must be prepared for it. I hope this book can help you, dear reader, to better understand what until now was impossible to be understood about this problematic, yet amazing, universe creation.

Atlan, 2019
Jan Val Ellam

BRIEF COMMENTARY

"Perhaps, more than any other time, we are facing ethical issues, but the answers don't come from an omniscient and peaceful heaven anymore. We are supposed to build them ourselves."
Hubert Reeves[1]

Are we alone in the universe?
Does God really exist? Is it possible to understand him?
What is the purpose of life?
Is there life after death?

Older people say that the 21st century will be known by the anguish that each one of us, Earth's inhabitants, will feel when trying to answer these five questions and so many others alike, after the occurrence of certain events.

Yes, I am talking about open and official visits from our cosmic brothers, partners in this adventure, which is to live in this universe.

When all people know it — even if this knowledge doesn't come through science but, in a first moment, through the occurrence of facts that will call the whole planet's attention – it won't be a matter of believing or not believing in religion's doctrines without deeply questioning them.

Each one will have to answer for oneself and, therefore, it will be necessary for all of us to dedicate ourselves to the art of self-development and evolution, independently of even having a religion.

In this book, we will try to explain what caused the Big Bang, what went wrong and also report a series of events that lead to the birth of Jesus on this planet, among other aspects of our unknown history.

Many feel hurt when asked to leave, even if only for a moment, the old dogmatic reaffirmations and enter a new path. If you are this kind of person, this book is not for you.

I must say that this work was built based on almost 40 books and hundreds of lectures that my father has done along more than 20 years of his life, with the assistance of extraterrestrial and extraphysical beings. His name is Jan Val Ellam, a pseudonym he chose before publishing his first book in 1996 called "Cosmic Reintegration".

We are beings that lost the notion of life's deepest sense and are limited only to our daily issues. In other words, we do not have a good understanding of the "big picture"!

Talking about the "big picture", let me use the parable of the bricklayers to better explain myself...

"Once, three bricklayers were working in the same civil construction. The three of them were executing the same job of laying bricks when someone passing by the construction asked the first one: What are you doing? The man answered promptly: I am laying bricks. The passer-by kept on walking and met the second worker, asking him the same thing. When he heard the question, he stooped for a while, looked around himself and said: I am laying bricks to build a big wall. At last, it was time for the passer-by to make the same question to the third worker: What are you doing? I am laying bricks to build a beautiful cathedral".

Three men doing the same job, however, three different answers to the same question.

The first man was only worried about his job and laying bricks seemed to be the best answer to give. That was his perception. The second one, before answering, stooped for a while and then concluded that to say he was laying bricks was kind of obvious and answered, since he found nothing better to say, he was building a wall. That was his perception of the job he was doing. The third worker, before beginning the hard work, decided to ask his boss if he could have a look at the project so that he could understand the purpose of his work. That's why he knew that his job of laying bricks was necessary to build a beautiful cathedral.

My anguish is: what if tomorrow someone asks me what I am doing… What am I going to say?

Well, I wake up every day and go to the university, then I go to work, after that, I come home and watch some TV, then I pray (asking for some stuff and saying thanks) and prepare myself to sleep.

On weekends and holidays I have fun with my friends going to the beach or I simply rest, sometimes I even work too. But what for? What difference am I making? I wonder if that is the purpose of life.

It's not that I don't like the life I have. On the contrary, sometimes I think I don't deserve to have such a wonderful life, especially in such an unequal world.

When I observe other people, I notice that regardless of being happy or sad with their lives, few try to discover what the purpose of the life we have on this planet is.

I believe that if like the third bricklayer, we put a little extra effort, we will also find out a bigger reason to exist and, this way, the laying of the bricks will have a new meaning.

I am sure it won't be an easy task!

One of the things that contribute the most to blocking our

perception of what is imperative to know, is our intellectual pride attached to convenience.

As a matter of fact, it's our pride that enables us to feel sympathy for those who have different points of view, religious ones or not.

I believe that if we are all living on the same planet, we may not be so different from each other in terms of nobleness and merit.

It is very easy, for example, to criticize the attitude of some politicians who are corrupt and are in search of money and power. However, which one of us can say that having been born in the same circumstances of these politicians, would act differently? I can't be sure about myself and I consider myself an honest man. In the same way, I can't be sure that if I were born in situations of extreme poverty I would not practice certain types of crimes to survive. I am not saying that poverty leads to criminality, but it definitely makes life harder to deal with.

Anyway, if you want it or not, if you like it or not, we are all exactly at the same level, spiritually speaking. We should not, therefore, claim to be better than anyone else, to know more than others, and to ridicule those who courageously try to stimulate our reasoning for things that need to be realized, regardless of religion.

Could it be that only what our poor five human senses can grasp is, in fact, the most important thing to be perceived? Isn't there a greater purpose for life incapable of being perceived by these five senses?

Is it smarter to believe that all the people who claim having seen a spirit or a flying saucer are lying or are mistaken than to believe in life after death or other intelligent life forms in the universe? If only one, among millions, is not lying or mistaken, it means it's true!

The facts do not suit our religions and our will so that we can understand them. We need to constantly analyze the concepts that we enthroned in our mind, as absolute and untouchable truths, to perceive certain aspects through more logical reasoning, less involved by beliefs.

To evolve it is necessary to renew concepts! Reinforcing the same thoughts will not make you change, therefore it will not help you evolve.

So, let's not be ashamed to break with old principles of religions which, although they comfort thousands of simpler humans, make millions of minds live stuck in concepts, without accepting anything that might hurt their beliefs.

Like Jan Val Ellam uses to say: "my religion is the religion of love. It is the same religion of Jesus, Siddhartha Gautama, Mohib Ibn Arab, Mother Teresa of Calcutta, Sathya Sai Baba and so many others".

Mohib Ibn Arab, a formulator of mystical Islam, known as the master of the masters, was perhaps the one who best translated the religion of love when he said, about 700 years ago:

"My heart has become capable of all things: it is pasture for the gazelles, a monastery for the monks and temple for the idols; is the Caaba for the pilgrims, the table of laws and the book of the Koran. My religion is the religion of love. Whatever path camels take, this is my religion and my faith".

I prefer to believe that all these wonderful men and women who have appeared on Earth have never intended to found any religion. Rather, they wanted to show the importance of discovering the purpose of life and teaching how to love unconditionally.

They were not meant to restrain anyone's reasoning. They wanted to create a new man and a new woman through the loving doctrine that should be the essence of all those who call themselves religious.

Too bad that everything becomes a matter of religion here on Earth, and we still do not love one another...

As we look at such beings, we have the distinct impression that it is impossible to imitate them, since they are true heroes. Maybe it's us that have gone crazy and we do not realize that their behavior is the same as all of us should have.

Life becomes more enjoyable when we reach the consciousness of fulfilling our role. Our role is fulfilled with harmony and naturalness when we adopt simplicity, forgiveness, empathy and loving practices. Our true nation is greater than the universe in all its dimensions.

It is logical to think that loving unconditionally should be the behavior of any minimally evolved cosmic citizen. It is not utopia. After all, not doing to others what you do not want to be done to you is trivial.

What was surprising for me was to find out that the ability to love is possible to be put into practice by the humankind, otherwise Jesus would probably not have been born here, as well as many other gurus have. Our DNA allows it!

I'm sorry to say that maybe the ability to love is not so easy to be found in this universe. We don't know, but we will eventually find out and we have to be prepared for all hypotheses. It is time to try to understand what is in reach for humankind, which is to understand the "big picture" about this universe and its creator.

But, coming back, who can convince a madman of his madness? These men and women tried to do it and were eventually persecuted, arrested, burned, and crucified. Their religious followers to this day have little changed regarding the essence of this monstrous behavior, and we do not even realize it. If our spirits had any idea in life how much we owe them all...

I hope our generation will not give up trying to love unconditionally in a world where those who dare to love are punished. Earth does not need heroes, it only needs daring men and women with a peaceful code of conduct, even if living in a violent world, in a problematic universe. Of course there is a price to be paid at the beginning, but we have to take the risk.

Enough of hypocrisy, religious nonsense enthroned as if it were precious!

We need to keep awake to the new and not to the old side of the cultural oddities that have always marked the careless walk of this humanity. We are citizens of the universe that, for now, inhabit the same planet.

Every person in this world needs to do what Gandhi said and did: to become an instrument of the change that wishes for this world.

If someone asks me what I am doing, I believe this is what I would answer: I am trying to fix the creation, managing my quota of electrons in a lucid, happy and loving way, trying to serve as an instrument to help those who need, preparing myself for the future and trying to evolve to be able to ascend to the highest spiritual levels when this body expires.

San Francisco, 2019
Rodrigo Freitas

1

THE MANY ABODES OF THE UNIVERSE

" *The hardness of our heart constitutes an obstacle to a definite and close contact with the aliens. The intellectual evolution enlightened by fraternal love, according to the teachings of Jesus, duly practiced, would enable us to receive the higher beings from other cosmic fields of the universe, to understand them and to assimilate the lessons of progress that could be ministered to us.*"

Francisco Cândido Xavier[1].

If I could guess the future and wanted to characterize the next ten years with just one word, I would say "spiritualization". With two words, I would say "cosmic reintegration".

Attention, I did not mean to become a spiritist. It is not necessary to change your religion, not even to have a religion. The important thing is to be spiritualized.

Seeking to connect Science and Spirituality by going over the pride that exists on both sides. Or will you tell me that you believe you're only made of flesh and blood? Don't you admit the existence of spirits?

Although there are hundreds of spiritual traditions around the world today, there are people who don't believe in spirits because they don't yet find the scientific proof they need to admit their existence, or simply because they can't see them.

Soon, I think we will all have a chance to know they exist and we will no longer need to believe or discredit. Spiritist mediums will be without jobs, because soon we must develop technological means, accepted by science and by all, to communicate with the disincarnated. For many people, **transcommunication**[2] is already a reality.

Some things become obvious, but science has not yet identified a proper way to prove it. Whatever! Even so, science is the most comfortable and safe territory to support our hypotheses about the truth that we are pursuing so much.

What **Allan Kardec**[3] did as a codifier of the Spiritist Doctrine in France was to use the empirical method to deduce and explain the intelligent cause behind the phenomena produced in Spiritist cults. The famous tables that answered questions from living men.

Science, even using the empirical method in some of its activities in biology and physics, does not admit the use of this method to prove the existence of spirits. What would be the method to use, I ask, before everyone simply starts seeing them to know they exist?

The universe we see is only part of the larger reality. What happens here will always be one of the possible options, according to the aspects of our existence, taking into account the limits imposed by the three-dimensionality of our level, allied to the time in terrestrial years.

We need to try to know more about the parallel realities that are inhabited by spirits, the diversity of environments and worlds that exist and we do not have access, or at least try to make sure they do not exist so we can discard this or that belief.

Imagine that after life on Earth, our spirit continues its journey in other dimensions. It would be strange to imagine, therefore, that there are extraterrestrials without spirit. Their spirit, according to the "Book of Spirits", in chapter four, is formed even in the same way as ours. We would, therefore, be cosmic brethren only wearing different bodily garments on the various worlds of the universe that are inhabited.

What matters is that every being must, in theory, possess a spirit, whether this being is on or out of the Earth, whether the spirit is the same or different from ours. Hence it is also concluded that the number of spirits must exceed those of incarnated beings, accounting for the so-called spiritual spheres, which are located inside our universe, around the worlds, but in other dimensions that are not the one of our planets and that our eyes can't see.

Have you ever imagined the size of the "mess"? Several worlds that, unlike ours, communicate with each other through mechanisms that we do not know, and also surrounded by spiritual environments! We know that it is difficult to conceive this vision because of all the limits that our physical and transient brain imposes, and also because we have been isolated from cosmic coexistence and we have lost the link with a time from our past in which we were not isolated.

Probably the vast majority of galaxies that men are identifying in the cosmos has many worlds inhabited by beings we do not know, sharing the material and spiritual side, perhaps in a much more evolved way than ours, but perhaps not. Perhaps they are older than us, but not necessarily more evolved in this regard.

We know nothing about anything on the spiritual side, though most people act as if they have nothing else to learn. The same applies to our beliefs regarding extraterrestrial life. It is incredible how our actions are unrelated to any concern with the spiritual context and its universal "rules".

Our little terrestrial brain seems to go crazy just by trying to imagine such a scenario. The words gain another context, for spiritually speaking there is no death. Science already knows that humans can't even use more than a small percentage of their physical brain. Which leads me to believe that we still have a long road ahead of evolution.

Jesus said that we should only seek to learn to love one another and everything else would be given to us in addition. Who knows if, deep down, he was telling us that to live in peace with all these other worlds, it is imperative that we live in peace on our own planet. Then we will be given a chance to perceive more than we have realized until now and develop other capabilities.

And who's worried about it in today's world? We know that the world's climate is "crazy," we fear the end of the world and the **final judgment**[4] and we know nothing about spirits or other civilizations from other worlds, not even about our past as a civilization of this planet.

Those who observe us from outside see us as inhabitants of Earth and not as Africans, Americans, Muslims, Catholics or anything else. If we do not manage our own diversity on the same planet, who imagines this possibility with citizens from other worlds?

Just the amount of murders and wars that have happened and still happen around here should scare any extraterrestrial civilization. Not to mention acts of gratuitous malice, rape, kidnapping, beatings, humiliation, blackmail and so on.

I know people who had to look at their girlfriend being raped without being able to do anything, friends who were victims of violent robberies inside their house and who lost almost everything, anyway, this is our planet! If you speak to any Brazilian, most of them will tell you they know people who have suffered some of these wildnesses. But it's not only in Brazil... By the time the bomb exploded on the train in Spain in 2004, I was taking a trip there and was on another train. It could have been in mine!

The mental habit of saying something like "thank you God because it was not in my train" is a criminal way to deal with a concept of God, in my opinion, but we often do that, and much more, because we were conditioned to do so.

Humiliation, aggression, drug trafficking, child trafficking, organ trafficking, animal trafficking, wars between nations, civil war, tribal wars, political scandals, attacks by extremist groups, kidnapping, public money evasion that should serve to avoid misery in the world... This all causes real traumas to the spirit and sometimes severe sequels during various incarnations, and we do not even know it while we are alive!

This would, therefore, be one of the reasons that could explain the fact that until today there has been no official and accepted record of contact with extraterrestrial intelligence. In fact, I believe that this is only part of the explanation and it's not the most important one.

To know all the reasons for this "cosmic isolation" that we face and to judge whether this is right or not, we would need to have access to our spiritual past and also to our ancient historical past here on Earth. We would also need to understand the reasons behind who ordered the cosmic isolation, because clearly they have been here in the past and they left, so something must have happened!

The problem is we do not seem to be really interested in that. Maybe we are afraid to find out the nonsense we must have done in other lives. If today the world is what it is, imagine when the technology and the laws were not like they are now. Feelings of guilt leave spiritual traumas that are hard to overcome.

We live as if something around here needs to happen, a kind of "love intervention," to get our attention and motivate us to evolve. After all, in our world, the only thing that matters is working to make money and having fun. If you can make money without working, even better!

We seem destined to live in a closed group, isolated from other worlds and other dimensions, in search for evolution and if we do not evolve urgently, we will destroy each other and the planet! We are at a critical moment in human history! Now, either we walk forward or the planet is over in a few decades.

For those who see us from the outside, like the aliens, I am convinced that there is no better definition for our planet than this: a crazy laboratory!

Here on Earth, we fear them even without knowing if they exist or not, and we produce films imagining battles with them, as if we had a chance to face them with our technology and as if they had some interest in destroying us. Analyzing well the facts of the earthly days, I would say that most of them probably have more than enough reasons to fear us.

It's us who are conditioned to lie, to steal, to be dishonest with each other, to kill, rape and so many other things that are part of the television newscast every day. And to make it worse, there are those who believe that this will never change! We find it difficult to imagine the world any other way. We are the "patients of the asylum/laboratory/jail" and it is important that we have this awareness so that we can be reintegrated into living with other civilizations.

In the next chapter, I will start introducing Jan Val Ellam's information about how this universe began to exist and what happened to its creator.

2

A BAD START

"The first world was destroyed as a punishment of bad actions done by man, by a consuming fire, which came from above and from below. The second world ended when the Earth globe leaned forward from its axis and everything was covered by ice. The third world ended in a universal flood. The present world is the fourth. Its fate will depend on whether or not its inhabitants behave according to the Creator's plans."
   Myth of the Hopi Indians[1].

We are creatures addicted to belief. Religion today is practically synonymous with truth for most of us.

It is indeed pleasant to think that our religions contain the knowledge of the truth, but it is time for us to reflect in an adult way. Reality is no hostage of human religions.

There is a reality that transcends our understanding. We are unprepared to understand it, and the worst, our spirits even after the death of our bodies, remain unprepared!

The shock that the immediate perception of a complex cosmic reality will cause in all religions and in the human being is inevitable, yet it will happen because it is necessary.

The inevitable encounter with reality and with the face of the truth that produced it is a matter of time, and there will be many encounters after the first official one.

The subject covered in this chapter is of extreme importance so that we can reflect on who we are, who God is (if He exists), where we come from, why we are on Earth (to this day without knowing officially if aliens exist) and how our situation looks after what the Bible calls the Last Judgment.

After all, as the myth of the Hopi Indians reminds us, there seem to have been historical periods when civilizations were wrecked by catastrophes of all kinds.

To understand our past as well as what the **doctrine of the Fallen Angels**[2] says and its great consequence for us, which ends up being the isolation from other civilizations of the universe, it is necessary for the reader to accept that human beings live a double life. One that is temporary, that is, transient, and another that is eternal and pre-existing. One is directly inserted into the other, whether we are aware of it while we are incarnate or not.

The temporary one would be, therefore, exactly the period in which we are now, where each of us is born, lives and "dies" in a world. The eternal is our spiritual life. It is as if, in a certain sense, time was an illusion, when the two are combined in one...

In order not to complicate much, let's just consider that we exist on Earth thanks to the union of two components: the physical body, which characterizes the human being and that we all know in-depth, and our spirit, which, despite having existed for much longer, is subject to the limits of the physical body to act in a universe.

In our case, these limits are the very limits of the human brain, which does not truly assimilate anything that does not come through the perception of our five senses: smell, sight, touch, hearing and taste; during the period in which this brain finds itself active.

Explaining better, we can say that although the physical body prevails throughout our lives on Earth, the capacity of the spirit is much greater. However, our spiritual capacities, for some reason, are asleep during life on Earth. That's why most human beings can't remember things that the physical brain has not witnessed, such as their past lives.

In particular, I believe that if we could remember in life our real universal cosmic identity, we would find it difficult to make friends and even choose our wives and husbands. Ultimately, the very reproduction of the human species would be a difficulty, since the history of our planet is fraught with complications in the sense of bad behavior committed to one another, and it would indeed be difficult to live with our former assassins, murderers of our relatives, former bosses and even with our husbands and wives of past lives. Anyway, it would probably be a disaster.

It is important the reader takes into account that, for over two thousand years, we must all have committed, as well as been victims of, a wide variety of types of violence. Millions of murders, bloody wars, city raids, rapes, injustices and humiliations in general. Let's not even talk about other planet's problems; just what happened and still happens on Earth is enough to illustrate what we are trying to say.

We have turned people like **Hitler, Stalin and Mao Tse Tung**[3] into real monsters, yet it's as if we have forgotten that alone they couldn't have done much.

Most of us have many unpleasant things in the spiritual baggage that are better left forgotten, otherwise we would be unable to evolve due to the strong feeling of guilt and life on Earth would probably be even more difficult.

The detail is that we live short lives, we use this "forgetfulness" to evolve, but what about a being who lives for billions of years? Believe it or not, according to Jan Val Ellam, many beings in this universe live billions of years!

Before this and any other universe was created, there was

what the kardecist spiritual revelation calls the **superior spirituality**.

This spiritual context will not be the focus of this work, but it is important to emphasize that, beyond the spiritual context linked to this universal physical creation, there is **superior spirituality**.

In **superior spirituality**, there are constant processes of creation. Whenever a creation occurs, **superior spirituality is shielded**.

This shield is created through a quantum collapse, to protect the **superior spirituality** of any type of contamination that may arise from some creation.

Using a reference from the **Brahmanda myth**[4], let's call the creation of this universe the "**cosmic egg**".

From this "cosmic egg" three things came:

1. Our physical universe, let's call it "**buhloka**";
2. The universe of antimatter, let's call it "**brahmaloka**"; and
3. A portion of the creator that created the "cosmic egg" in the first place, let's call it (not him, not her) "**Brahma**".

The name of Brahma may change, but many mythologies of ancient cultures claim that our "Big Bang" came about this way. Religions have distorted this history. Other names of the creator of the "cosmic egg" are: Yahweh, Allah, Chaos, Pangu, among several others. Brahma is the one used in the Hindu tradition. **Vishnu and Shiva are the other two gods of the Hindu Trimurti** and we will talk about all three of them.

So, the only being that existed in the "cosmic egg" at that time was a fallen part of the creator himself.

For billions and billions of years, the "buhloka" has developed lifeless. Life first appeared in the "brahmaloka" from clones engendered by the creator in the beginning. We will better tell this story along this work.

Before the first generations of clones were created, the only spirit that was in some way conveyed to this creation was the one of Brahma. While his real spirit fainted in **superior spirituality**, a mental portion was shielded within the "cosmic egg", more precisely within the "brahmaloka".

The story that we will reveal with this work is not intended to be taken as truth, but it must be analyzed by whoever wants to understand what until today could not be understood through religions. When Earth gets reintegrated into the cosmic coexistence with other civilizations, the things we are talking about here will be very important to understand what will be going on.

The romantic idea that God has prepared a special and perfect place to create humanity is a distorted view of truth.

The "cosmic egg" was created in a problematic way and also the concept of God should not be confused with the one of the universal creator(s). It was indeed a bad start!

Brahma is not a perfect being like God should be, he is only a sick portion of the mind of the real spirit of Brahma, who is also not God.

That is why when reading the Bible, one can tell that there is something weird with the biblical "God" Yahweh (or Jehova). Its sickness and the problems of its creation will be presented in future chapters of this work.

So, **superior spirituality** contains everything, nothing can be created outside of it because there is no outside of it! A quantum collapse shields the creations, as mentioned before. **Superior spirituality** has always existed and, of course, it is hard for the human being to understand something that has always existed.

Low spirituality (or operational spirituality) is the one linked to the creation. It was generated after life came to exist in this "cosmic egg", because the spirits that had to jump into this creation had to use some kind of body, and could not simply return to **superior spirituality**, when and if these bodies expired. These spirits got "trapped" in bodies that last for billions and billions of years!

At first, Brahma was the only living consciousness in the "cosmic egg". In the first millennia, after regaining his composure, he was able to create other beings as well. Let's call them "clones of Brahma", but we could also call them angels, like the Bible does.

The first spirits that jumped into the "cosmic egg" were not simple and ignorant spirits, like the ones that would appear later on. They were spirits who decided to plunge into this creation to help the fallen creator. It was a kind of divine favor. What father or mother would not do the same to rescue a son or a daughter? They dove in for love.

For now, let's just understand that operational spirituality was created to support the spirits that have plunged into this universe. It has several sublevels and each one has its kind of shield.

After the Talm Project implementation, which will be analyzed in a specific future chapter of this book, the biological beings came to exist in the "buhloka" and further intensified the traffic between **superior spirituality** and operational spirituality.

From then on, many simple and ignorant spirits came to exist as individualized consciousnesses transiently occupying biological bodies in the "buhloka". **Sophia**[5] was the first being to live in the "buhloka", and this only took place around 5 billion years after the BIG BANG.

Low spirituality, or operational spirituality, was developed by the very spirits imprisoned by the shield caused by the quantum collapse that ensures there is no possibility of contamination of the **superior spirituality**.

For instance, there are many different spiritual cities

surrounding our planet and when our bodies expire, most of us will go there, before going anywhere else.

Our individualized consciousness can only go to other universes, or even return to **superior spirituality,** if they are immaculate.

This version of the truth could not be taken seriously until now because of our degree of religious affiliation. In order to minimize our degree of ignorance regarding this spiritual context, here on Earth, we had some attempts from spirits that were organized in operational spirituality. We can and should here highlight Allan Kardec's work in this regard. However, once again our religious-minded behavior has turned his work into another religion, but that is another story that will have to be addressed another time.

The clones, as well as other species that were created in the "brahmaloka", simply live long lives. Billions of years! What we call angels here on Earth are really clones of Brahma.

The concept of an angel is ingrained in all earthly religions, as well as the concept of God, and Demons. To understand the information in this book, we need to reread the meaning of these terms, of these expressions.

There was a time, before the religions, where these concepts were much closer to the cosmic reality. Ancient cultures believed there were good and bad angels, good and bad gods, good and bad demons.

In this problematic creation, there are 3 beings that use to call themselves Gods: Brahma, Shiva and Vishnu. They have created the other species that live in the "brahmaloka".

For now, we will call these species angels and demons and we will try to better conceptualize these species, although it is very difficult to do that because they are completely different from human beings.

Angels are the clones of Brahma. They are mostly robotized and few have managed to evolve to free themselves from the imprisonment of their own bodies. Their abilities to reason are limited by the desires of Brahma and they live to serve their creators commands.

Today we may think that angels are good and demons are bad, but this has nothing to do with the truth.

Demons are beings that emerged later on when Shiva and Vishnu also started creating beings. They also have low abilities to reason, they compete among themselves and most of them can metamorphose.

Brahma cannot be judged as being good or bad and nor can any of the species that live in the "brahmaloka". Whatever they are, it is completely different from the biological beings of the "buhloka". Some have good intentions but others are less evolved and can represent what we would classify as being bad or evil. We, humans, are the same! Some can be called good humans and some can be called bad humans.

Brahma did not always create his clones in an intentional and planned way. Especially in the beginning, he saw himself as a conscious being but who commanded several scattered parts. These parts later evolved and became their clones, acting under his command, trying to organize the environment of the "brahmaloka".

After the first billions of years had passed, one of these clones made a move against Brahma's will and assaulted him. It was the first time Brahma realized there was another consciousness working side by side with him in his creation. **Let's call Shiva this aggressor clone**.

Shiva was at first a clone of Brahma who dove into this universe out of love for the creator. But inside the creation, the only way for him to exist was to occupy one of these bodies that we are calling clones.

It was only over time that the spirit of Shiva was able to perform its own action which was precisely to attack Brahma, so that he would stop creating other generations of problematic beings.

For Brahma, it was like his hand decided to punch him in the head. Until then, this concept of "the other" for him did not exist. And for millennia he reorganized himself to annihilate the aggressor clone.

When Brahma finally succeeded, there arose the first being that we can classify as a demon in this creation. The spirit of Shiva resurfaced within Brahma's "brahmaloka" as the **first demon** and started to dispute with Brahma over the control of the universe. Demon here only means a different kind of being if compared to the clones. It does not mean good or bad, as we have already said.

The communication was a problem since then, and apparently, the only way to fix this creation was to face Brahma in a dispute. Brahma never really understood that Shiva was trying to help him fix the creation, or at least finish it without creating even bigger problems.

So Shiva was a clone who became a demon, but could only do so by losing his clone body, which Brahma destroyed. Shiva's spirit has a lot of difficulties to communicate with Shiva, just like today our spirit has a lot of difficulties to communicate with our transitory personalities.

As we said, the demon body was different from the clones. Shiva created several generations of demons to be able to obey his commands and dispute with Brahma and his clones. And all of this happened in the "brahmaloka".

As much as they had tried, Brahma and Shiva realized in the midst of their disputes that they could not completely destroy one another and so they kept on disputing until a third being emerged in the creation from the descendants of Shiva. **Let's call this being Vishnu.**

Vishnu did not emerge as a robotic clone of Brahma. He

emerged as a demon of Shiva and this made it easier for him to free his mind from Brahma and Shiva.

Vishnu also had amazing powers and created generations of demons. So, the three of them disputed and assaulted each other for a long time, until they all realized they could not destroy each other.

At this point, they sliced the "brahmaloka" so they could live together and each generation of clones and demons began to inhabit a "loka" specially developed within the "brahmaloka". Each one of the three "Gods" had its own "loka" and also each generation had its own "lokas". By the way, the meaning of "loka" would be "abode". In Greek they use the word "genos".

What we can call "Lila" is another term in Sanskrit which means the play of disputes and bets of these three "Gods".

The "Lila" started at this point and lasted until around the year 2016 according to Jan Val Ellam revelations. The story of how the "Lila" stopped will be analyzed at another moment.

During the first billion years of this creation, while the confusing reality of the "Lila" was going on in the "brahmaloka", in the "buhloka" only the generations of stars were succeeding and producing complex chemical elements, but there was still no life.

The first of these chemical elements in the "buhloka" was the hydrogen. From the succession of stars that were born and died, the other elements that we know today started arising.

Only in the third generation of stars the heaviest chemical elements that make up the planets and our biological bodies begin to emerge, and this took about five billion years.

When, after billions of years of disputes, some of these demons realized that they all failed and the "brahmaloka" also failed, the strategy now known as "Talm Project" began to be idealized and put into practice. We will talk more about the Talm Project along this book.

3

AFFECTED REASONING AND COSMIC IGNORANCE

"I can not believe in a God who wants to be praised all the time..."
Friedrich Nietzsche[1]

Since I was a child I have heard of a being who lived on Earth about two thousand years ago, and I learned to have respect for him because I realized that although people had different religious opinions, they usually admired and praised him.

The doctrine says he was the son of God, an advanced spirit who was born, lived and died, crucified as we all know. This man was able to walk on water, multiply food, heal the sick only with his love and even reanimate a dead person.

Trying to imagine how I would behave if I had all this power, I came to the conclusion that Jesus really ought to be a highly evolved person, far above the earthly average. Even though he had the power to snap his "enemies", he preferred to die humiliated and tortured, nailed to a cross.

If it were me with these powers, I would probably have dominated the world and lived as the Earth Kings live: full of slaves, eating and drinking the best food available and living in a palace, while the rest of the people starve and struggle to survive.

Instead, this man allowed himself to be killed and, before dying, he still asked his "Loving Father" or whatever name we want to use, to have mercy on his murderers, and on all of us on a closer look because we did not know what we were doing. We did not know anything back then, and we continue not knowing much about his "Loving Father".

Time passed, I grew older and kept hearing about Jesus. In school, on the street, in churches, in spiritist centers, on television, in books... Anyway, Jesus was everywhere!

It is believed that Jesus was a man who was born into a humble family and that his mother, Mary, was a virgin. An angel introduced himself to her and told her that her future son would simply be the "messiah" awaited by all the Jewish people, sent by the Jewish God.

I think she believed in the angel since she got pregnant despite not having had sexual intercourse until then... But that, although extraordinary, is not difficult for us to believe nowadays since now we all understand what artificial insemination is, but that's not very important. What is essential is that the being that would divide the history of the Earth was born; the "messiah" expected by the Jewish people and prophesied by so many, including **John the Baptist**![2]

During his life, Jesus spoke and did things that his friends, apostles and family could not understand. Jesus said, among other things, that his kingdom was not of this world, that wielding a sword could not sow love, that there are many abodes in the house of the Father, that he did not intend to change the course of the law, nor to take positions of government, that he was not on Earth to remove the vigorous men from their occupations and that, first of all, only the Father was perfect.

No one understood anything, not even the apostles and family. Two thousand years have passed and we still do not understand much!

The incredible thing is that even representing the ideal of all of us in our desire to evolve spiritually, Jesus made a point of saying that **only the Father is perfect.**

It is even difficult to imagine such a perfect being, but according to Jesus, this being exists.

The great question of this chapter is: Is the God described in the Bible, in the old testament, the same perfect "Loving Father" that Jesus spoke about so much?

Of course not! The God of the old testament is the creator, known as Brahma, Allá, Yahweh, Jehova and many other names.

According to Genesis, which is the first book of the Bible, God, in creating man and placing him in the Garden of Eden, told him that he could eat fruits of all trees except the tree of the knowledge of good and evil, because the day he ate, he would die. The woman, after a conversation with the "serpent", decided to eat the fruit and gave it to her husband. Not one of them died after eating the fruit... God, displeased with both, then throws a curse on the serpent, the woman, and the man, and expels them from paradise. God...? Lying to humans and handing out curses? I believe that a minimally spiritualized man would not curse anyone, why would God do it? The only explanation is that what the Bible calls God is being confused with the figure of the creator of this specif creation, called Yahweh.

Then Adam and Eve, now cast out of paradise, have their first two sons: Cain and Abel. When they were older, both of them decided to make offerings to God; however, God liked only Abel and the offer made by him. How is such a thing possible? God liked one and did not like the other? Cain, jealous thanks to the attitude of God, kills his younger brother and also receives a curse!

After all, what God is this who creates man and forbids him to eat the fruit of knowledge, lies when telling him that he would die if he ate the fruit, expels him from paradise, throws a curse upon him, and further causes jealousy in Cain, despising his offering? Neither I, with all my faults, think I would act this way.

Further on, continuing to read the Genesis, God saw that Earth was corrupted and that men had been responsible for it. He decides, then, to exterminate from the face of the planet the men he created together with the animals. However, the only man who got the love of God was Noah, and so he was asked to build an ark to save his family and a couple of every kind of animal on Earth. God then casts the flood and kills all the rest that was not inside the ark. How generous!

Earth was then repopulated from the descendants of Noah. God now decides, it is not known why, to confuse the language of men so that one does not understand the language of the other. That's what I call a divine attitude!

I could go on and on about it...

To finish my point, in addition to requiring a three-year-old heifer, a three-year-old goat, a three-year-old lamb, a dove, and a pigeon, God then commands Abraham to circumcise all the boys when they complete eight days to mark the chosen people of the perpetual covenant established in exchange for lands, descendants, and protection. What God was thinking when he made this covenant is what I ask myself.

Continuing the Biblical reading, God decides to destroy the cities of Sodom and Gomorrah since only sinners were living in these cities...

Then, God asks Abraham to kill his son. At the very moment when Abraham was about to kill his son Isaac, an angel stopped him and said that since Abraham had not denied God his own son, he would bless him and save Isaac's life. Now God knew that Abraham really feared Him.

What kind of God is the one who wants to be feared by us and who has to do tricks like this to know the nature of people?

What God is this one who needs offerings, who loves to be feared and who curses all the time? If the God who is described in Genesis and in most of the Bible is not the same one whom

Jesus spoke so much about, who would then be the God of the Bible? As we said, it can only be the creator of the "cosmic egg"!

I do not mean that the information contained therein is silly or false. That's not it. I take the Bible very seriously! Probably more than most religious who apparently don't truly believe in what they read, and worse, don't think about what they read. Let's see what Jan Val Ellam brings us in terms of explanations...

If we want to understand the truth and purpose of our existence, we must think, not just believe. We should read books of all possible religions, but we should not be embarrassed to question anything. If sacred dogmas only serve to be believed, then they do not serve for much.

After all, do the sacred dogmas of Catholicism, Judaism and Islamism, among other "isms", embellish the world? It was with the excuse of defending these dogmas that followers of these religions practiced and practice many crimes! Thankfully, nowadays I can no longer go to the stake of the Inquisition, for it was only a few years ago that this could happen to anyone who wrote something that would displease the Church.

The example of what, here on Earth, comes closest to the concept of what God can be, in my modest opinion, is the legacy that men like Jesus and some others offered us.

So, using Jan Val Ellam's explanations, who is Jesus? Jesus is a homo sapiens personification of a spirit from the **superior spirituality**. He has proven that a divine spirit can be a God if embodied in a biological homo sapiens body.

What is intriguing is that, at the same time, this same spirit could not be considered what we would call a God when embodied in other kinds of bodies, created before the biological species. The best one was definitely Jesus!

His spirit is able to act in (or support) several kinds of bodies at the same time, no matter if these bodies are in the "buhloka" or in the "brahmaloka".

Jan Val Ellam calls this kind of spirit **"addhy"**. It is different from our spirit because we can only support a single ego at once. We have had several lives before this one, but each one at a time, not several at the same time.

We will analyze some of his other personifications later, but here we can mention a few of them: **Vishnu, Mohen So and Sophia, among several others** that had to be created both in the "brahmaloka" and in the "buhloka". Jesus was the last one of them and the closest to what we can call a God.

The "brahmaloka" is the universe of the long lives. Life started with Brahma and his clones and only after a certain amount of around 6,1 billion years life was created in the "buhloka", as we mentioned at the end of the previous chapter.

The clones, as well as other species that were created there, simply live long lives. Billions of years!

The "buhloka" is the universe of shorter lives. For instance, we, homo sapiens, live around 80, maybe 100 years only.

The homo sapiens are too recent, from only 200 thousand years ago. Now compare it with the age of both universes, the Science calls it the BIG BANG, which happened 13.8 billion years ago. 200 thousand years is nothing compared to that.

It seems homo sapiens might just be the most recent biological species that emerged in the "buhloka", and according to Jan Val Ellam, that is exactly the case!

Jesus promised to come back in the future, but he will do that as Sophia, another personification of the same spirit. Sophia would be his "glorified body" which as made to last until the end of "buhloka".

Actually, Sophia was the first being created in the "buhloka" and he is completely different if you compare it to Jesus or any other of his personifications. Although we are talking about the same spirit, it is different from our spirit, and it can take care of more than one universal personification, as we have just mentioned.

There are a few other spirits in a mission in the "cosmic egg" that can do the same thing, but Brahma is NOT one of them. The spirit of Brahma remains fainted in **superior spirituality** while Jesus spirit acts and develops his plans to deal with the difficulties of acting inside the "**cosmic egg**" **universes**.

Sophia was created to exist until the end of this creation, Jesus was not! Brahma, or Yahweh, or Allá is the god of the old testament and believe it or not, he exists! He is not the perfect "Loving Father" who Jesus mentioned, although we need to go a lot deeper if we want to understand what really happened and why Jesus had to be crucified. And we will try to do that on this book, especially on the sixth chapter, but first we have to try to explain things a little better.

4

THE ROLE OF RELIGIONS AND ITS SACRED BOOKS

"I live surrounded by priests and priests, who say that their kingdom is not of this world. However, they grab everything they can."
    Napoleão Bonaparte[1].

"The more I study religions, the more I convince myself that men have never worshiped anything but themselves."
    Sir Richard Francis Burton[2].

I remember the day when I went to confess to the priest so that I could make the first eucharist. After all, my grandparents and my parents got married in the church and this is the tradition in the city I grew up. I was seven years old and had to invent some "sins" to tell the priest; such as swearing during soccer matches, so he could tell me what I should pray and then be forgiven by God. When I asked him if Jesus was God or his son, honestly I don't remember what he answered, but I remember it did not convince me...

The funny thing is that later on, during that day, I had time to play soccer, play video games, and the result is that bad words kept coming out... Every time I said a bad word I would think "Forgive me Jesus" to try to nullify the "Sin" that I had just committed. Sometimes I would even pronounce the words very low... How innocent I was!

Nowadays, I wonder what is the great sin a seven-year-old child can do. In my view, we should not hold a seven-year-old child accountable for "invented sins," as well as passing on the idea that we should fear God. We should rather seek to educate children by teaching the importance of seeking to love one another.

Children can only commit "sins" if those who are in charge of educating them - that is, family, school, and church - are completely irresponsible. Sin, I believe in a general way, must be the evil we do to others intentionally or irresponsibly and that is what must be understood by seven-year-old kids.

The problem is that in today's world, there aren't many people who are daughters and sons of balanced and correct mothers and fathers in everyday life. Many grow up without a father or a mother to educate them. It's hard to be a right citizen if your parents did not give you love. And one who loves, educates.

Few are also those who have the opportunity to study in good schools and universities and who seize this opportunity. Finally, religions that should serve to educate children within a doctrine of loving life and one another, as well as making them free to act ethically and according to one's own conscience during one's life, teaching the importance of trying to love unconditionally, are basically concerned only with disputing and keeping believers.

Returning... Older, I discovered that something similar had happened to some friends and also to my father when he was being prepared to make his first eucharist decades before me. Did the same thing happen to you?

I, a seven-year-old boy, was a sinner! What a violence with the reasoning of a child! The priest, on the other hand, would be someone so powerful that, after I pray some "Lord's Prayer" and some "Hail Marys" as he told me to, I would be saved and therefore free to do the first eucharist.

I do not believe that a human being needs a religion to exercise his cosmic citizenship. It is not necessary. The number of people who believe they are getting rid of hell by attending a weekly mass or by receiving passes is unbelievable. There are also those who pay a certain percentage of what they receive to the churches. These are sure that they can demand from God a place in heaven!

Bishops and priests, who are sometimes also deputies, senators, or other kinds of politicians, are the ones who need our money, not God. There is no worst blind than the one who does not want to see. No one needs an intermediary to "talk to God". That can not be the role of the Church, nor should it ever have been.

The problem with religions is that the essential thing, which is to inspire people to improve individually, based on the attitude of loving without requiring anything in return, seems to be forgotten.

How do we stay then? Is religion good or bad?

It depends a lot on how people view the religion they follow. It would be better if we all loved each other and had no religion. We would feel free to disagree... The best conclusion may be that religions may, under certain circumstances, contribute in certain aspects, but may also worsen people's psychological state, and as the planet acquires knowledge, religious movements tend to fall into disrepute along with their dogmas and sacred beliefs.

I must say that, in my opinion, religions, as they are currently practiced, serve to divide the world into rival groups, so that the believers can not love their neighbors if they belong to other groups. Everyone has to learn how to think for themselves and not to simply believe in what a priest, a pastor or a medium might say.

Human pride is something so strong that when someone says that we are wrong about our religion, we immediately put on a defensive psychological armor and we defend ourselves rather than defend the truth - whatever it is. Often this makes it impossible for us to love our neighbors and even makes communication between people unpleasant. How silly!

The great gap of religions is that their leaders are, with very few exceptions, imperfect men like all of us, but who dictate rules of reasoning and defend their ideals of the "attacks" of other "believers" from other religions.

Their pride blinds them to the point of believing that someone has the power to "heal" someone from their respective sins... As long as the sinner repents and attends the religious determined rites and rituals, not forgetting, of course, to leave a "contribution".

We should not believe that religious fanatics are just Muslims. This is stupidity! Christianity, for example, has outgrown Islam in terms of logical absurdities and atrocities towards other human beings throughout history. **Jan Huss**[3], **Giordano Bruno**[4] and many others who say so!

Religious fanatics are easy to find anywhere in the world, and I'm not talking about modern terrorists... I'm talking about people who are narrow-minded and believe in what they stand for as absolute truth, even if they do not understand it!

It is not possible to go back in time, and if it was through religion that men could not completely forget the example of beings like Jesus, while he was incarnated and living the transience on our planet, then today we are suffering the consequences of this path.

In this context, if religions are based on the sacred books, another question that must be asked is: what is the function of these books? For us westerners, it is almost impossible to stop talking about the Bible. We do not intend to address all the seventy-three books that compose it now, that will be, perhaps, for an upcoming job. For the moment we will be content to discuss only certain parts and also certain indispensable aspects for those who are interested in the subject.

The origin of the Bible, so often mentioned by believers and Catholics, seems to be ignored by most people, and this is a fact that harms those who try to discuss and understand it without necessarily being bound to any religion. Knowing the Bible by heart is no use, we must try to understand it as an incomplete and imperfect source of information. It is not the word of God!

To start, there is no scientific certainty of who would have written all forty-six books of the Old Testament. The Jews believe that Moses would have been the author of the first five books that are: Genesis, Exodus, Leviticus, Numbers, and Deuteronomy, which is accepted by most religions.

In the New Testament, the twenty-seven books are twenty-one epistles or letters, four gospels that are those of Matthew, Mark, Luke, and John (there is no proof that they actually wrote them), the Acts of the Apostles and the Apocalypse, which is precisely what refers to the promise that Jesus would have made to return to Earth in the future, and is consequently the most important to understand what is happening and also what is about to happen (by John, the same from the Gospels).

In fact, it is known that the Bible we know today is the result of a selection work performed by a genial priest of Rome called **Jerome**[5]. Great because it should not have been easy to select the seventy-three books, among hundreds of books of the Jewish people and thousands that existed about Jesus. It is believed that by the end of the second century after Christ there were about four thousand gospels! Great also because of the way in which such a selection was made, the essence of Jesus' work was transmitted and, at the same time, Jerome was able to soften the guilt of the romans upon his death and exalt the jewish people's, after all, he was a priest of Rome and to clear the romans was also part of his task.

That's right. The Bible may be full of mysteries, but at the same time it is just the result of this work and should not be seen as a perfect book without fails, but as a great source of study which, if studied together with other great sources of other religions and with the aid of science and spirituality, can help us to unravel what happened in our past and to understand a larger context that surpasses existence on Earth.

It can help us understand who we are and why we are living on this planet. It can even contribute to breaking certain paradigms such as the one of religion and science being adversaries.

When I first read the Bible as a source of study and not as a book of absolute and complete truths, the first impression I had was that any science fiction film, as crazy as it may be, should not get even close to having the amount of madness that our planet must have witnessed in the past!

If we want to discover the truth about our past we have to analyze all these "follies" and "myths" with religious impartiality, considering the time and the author of the scriptures. Not forgetting to interpret things according to a larger context that seems plausible, given the impossibility of greater confirmation by science.

With that in mind, let's go back and talk about the first book of the Bible which is Genesis. Some of the most important facts described in Genesis are:

- The myth of Creation - which among the most important facts of Genesis is perhaps the most important.
- The divine genealogy that links Adam to Abraham - and later Abraham to Jesus in the New Testament.
- The interference of the Neflims - which the Sumerians called the Anunnaki and who are actually extraterrestrial beings - are discussed in chapter five of

this book and have much to do with the myth of
Creation.

- The Garden of Eden - the place from which the man
  and the woman were expelled.
- The story of Enoch - who disappeared from Earth
  taken to the heavens without dying, returned to Earth,
  wrote his books and then was taken to heaven again. It
  is important to note that Enoch and Elijah are the two
  men who never died, but were both "taken to heaven".
- And, finally, Sodom and Gomorrah.

That is, only in this single book of the Bible, we can already
see several of these "follies" to which I referred, and know that
only a few were mentioned.

On the creation myth, it is written that on the first day God
created the light so that day and night could exist, on the second
day he created the sky, on the third day he created the Earth, the
vegetation and the sea, in the fourth he created the sun, moon
and other stars of the firmament, in the fifth he created life in
water and birds, in the sixth he created the living beings of the
Earth, as well as man and woman, and on the seventh day he
rested.

Interestingly, over a century ago, the writing of certain tablets,
discovered in the ruins of ancient Mesopotamia and belonging to
the Sumerians, was deciphered.

It was then realized that certain tablets related to the biblical
creation myth a millennium before the Old Testament was
composed, which begins exactly with the Genesis. So, whatever is
described in there is, in fact, a copy of a part of the ancient texts
of the Sumerians!

What is even more interesting is that whenever our modern
science advances to the point of obtaining a satisfactory answer
about our planetary origin, it adapts itself to Sumerians and
confirms it.

The Sumerians already knew for six thousand years, and with scientific accuracy, facts that science has been discovering and verifying nowadays. Madness? No, it's just facts!

Let us now speak a little of the Sumerians to understand how this is possible...

5

HAS HUMANITY KNOWN ABOUT THE EXISTENCE OF ETS?

"... I was overwhelmed by the irresistible feeling that the Nile Valley was the scene of important events for humanity, long before the documented history of humanity began. All the ancient records and traditions of Egypt speak of these facts and link us to a time when the gods reigned on Earth: the fabulous First Times, which were called Zep Tepi."
Graham Hancock[1]

I remember that in my high school years, where we students were being prepped for college entrance, some history teachers spoke about the Sumerians. They said that it was a people whose origin is unknown, up to the present day, and lived about 6,000 years ago, at least, in ancient Mesopotamia, in a region called Sumeria that would be located in the south of current Iraq.

They were also said to be an extremely advanced people who recorded their commercial and legal transactions, as well as their tales and stories in clay tablets.

After the college preparation year, I never heard of Sumerians again until I was presented with a book called *Genesis Revisited* written by **Zecharia Sitchin**[2].

This book shows us, based on scientific studies and

statements of respected names of science, that most of the great scientific discoveries of the last years were already known in the ancient Sumerian civilization, thanks to the intervention of extraterrestrial colonizers!

This is not just a hypothesis; it is simply the translation of what is written on the tablets!

Madness? Translation error? Madness is not admitting the existence of aliens! It is time to stop treating the extraterrestrial issue as crazy stuff.

It is not known with certainty which was the first people from which the history of humanity began. Some think it was from the Sumerians themselves. The truth is that science is always discovering evidence of the existence of other extremely ancient civilizations (probably predating the Sumerians) elsewhere in the world, such as in South America itself. But let's leave this controversy aside. The important thing here will be to address some points regarding the knowledge of the Sumerians.

In the previous chapter we were talking about Genesis and the creation myth, described early in the Bible, which seems to be a summary copy of the content contained in the Sumerian tablets, which were written at least millenniums before the birth of Jesus.

According to scholars of the subject, for example, the writer L.W. King, there are at least seven Sumerian tablets dealing with creation. Six contained the process of creation itself and one that only exalted God, the Creator. "Coincidentally," according to Genesis, the world was created in seven "days," being six of work and one of rest.

"At the beginning,
God created heaven and earth.
The Earth was empty,
Darkness covered the abyss
And a wind of God hovered over the waters.
God said, "Let there be light"; and there was light.
God saw that the light was good And God separated the light
from the darkness: The Light God called the day, and the
darkness he called the night. There were an afternoon and a
morning: it was the first day."
Genesis 1:1

We can say that one of the great goals of Biblical Genesis is to clarify to the reader just how our planet originated. I said "just" because it does not address the creation of the solar system.

The Sumerian texts begin even before the creation of our planet. The conclusion is that what is described in the Bible is only the part that refers directly to the emergence of the planet Earth, in the way we currently consider it, and which is only part of what is described in the tablets.

The Nephilim, who are also mentioned in the biblical texts, which the Sumerians called the Anunnaki, are exactly the inhabitants of another planet called Nibiru. Crazy.... don't you think?

To help the reader understand the importance of all this and give a little credit to this fact, it is worth mentioning a great detail: until 1986, scientists thought that the constitution of Uranus, a planet in the solar system that was discovered only in 1781, would probably be similar to the giants Jupiter and Saturn, that is, a yellow-brown planet and gaseous.

Thanks to Voyager 2, it was discovered in 1986 that Uranus was actually surrounded by water in its atmosphere and its color was blue-green. Totally different than was imagined.

The incredible thing is that the Sumerians not only knew of

the existence of this planet, but they also knew its characteristics, and yet they left in writing the record that Uranus was blue-green and watery, about six thousand years ago in its tablets! The modern world did not know this information until 1986!

How is this possible? Simple: the information was brought in from outside by an extraterrestrial civilization, the Nephilim, which also appears in the Bible. Again, that's what it says on the tablets!

If it were not for extraterrestrials, the other chances would be, or the Sumerians had telescopes much more modern than the present ones or they had space ships. According to our historical perspective, none of these hypotheses seems to have been possible, technologically speaking, for at least a few thousand years before the birth of Jesus.

Therefore, it does not seem to me precipitate to conclude that the extraterrestrials have already been here! On the contrary, it seems logical! This leads me to think that some parts of the Bible that refer to God should actually refer to extraterrestrial entities.

According to Jan Val Ellam, that is precisely the case. The creator of the universe, according to the Bible, God, also created the humans and everything else but in fact, the humans were a product of manipulations performed by several extraterrestrial beings from different civilization groups. We could mention specially the Anunnakis and some beings from "Brahmaloka".

If they do exist, we may also conclude that it is only a matter of time before Earth receives again a visit from them, or visits…

For some reasons which are being discussed in this book, until today we are not sure, scientifically speaking, even if they do exist.

What has happened throughout our history so that, nowadays, the extraterrestrial factor is something that is disregarded by us? Why haven't they simply shown themselves clearly in these last two thousand earthly years?

Understanding the reason why it was not possible to make

direct and official contact with extraterrestrial intelligence to this day should be the great questioning of scholars and even of science! Just knowing they exist would change us a lot, and it takes a lot of effort not to admit they were here in the past.

If, indeed, they were here - and the ancient holy books, such as the Bible, the **Book of the Dead**[3], the **Mahabaratha**[4] and the **Popol Vuh**[5], among others, state that they were - why no clear and open contact has yet been made?

The cosmic context of this universe, its creator and his assistants, life on Earth and other planets... The big picture is so incredibly unpleasant and complex that it's almost unbelievable.

6

WHAT IS RESERVED FOR US?

"We need to work hard to end the isolation of Earth, and to make our philosophical principles activated by our existential responsibility and not by belief." **Jan Val Ellam**

The most important concept for understanding the moment Earth is currently experiencing is "cosmic reintegration", that is, the perspective that we will be able to coexist with intelligence that is not of this planet. And this should occur in the coming days, months or years, but it won't take long, according to Jan Val Ellam.

No one knows the day, but it will come!

The inhabitants of the planet, generally, regardless of religion or any other aspect, must learn certain principles of a kind of "universal law" that governs everything and everyone that is inserted in the cosmos.

It is in this "law" that spirits of the size of **Zoroaster**[1], **Siddhartha Gautama**[2], Jesus and so many other masters who lived on Earth are graduates.

If we can't follow their examples or even misrepresent their philosophies of life with our attitudes on a daily basis, turning everything into religious issues, it's our problem.

The central point of reflection is that, whether we are prepared or not, we who will live a few more years incarnated in this world, will see and witness the process of cosmic reintegration in its most precious moment, which will be the moment when we will receive the visit of the entity that, on Earth, became known as Jesus, and in the cosmos is known as Sophia. Cosmic reintegration means, in fact, the end of the isolation that began about five thousand years ago and lasts until now.

It is important to realize that, behind our eyes, there is a whole spiritual question that we do not know as incarnate - and which we desperately need to begin to notice - although we all continue to act as if we do not need to learn anything regarding this matter, as we have already said. We live as if all "things of the world" are more important than the spiritual essence of life, which presupposes the constant improvement of each one of us.

Faced with this fact, one might even wonder: how important is a personal improvement if the rest of the universe appears to be extremely problematic?

In the early 1960s, some Japanese scientists studied various groups of monkeys that lived on small islands in the Japanese archipelago. They would go on boats, throw potatoes for the monkeys, go to another island and throw the potatoes for the monkeys of that other island. They went out daily throwing the potatoes for the monkeys on all the islands.

Detail: the monkeys on one island could not see the others. Usually, the monkeys would pick up the dirty dirt potatoes and eat it. One day, the scientists realized that a young female took the potato and washed in the seawater, taking out the dirt before eating.

The next days they realized that, besides that little female, two or three other monkeys were doing the same. Over time, they found that almost the entire population of that island had taken on the new habit. Amazingly, when an X number of monkeys on that island also began to automate that habit, the other monkeys on the other islands began to do the same thing.

Then came the theory that defines the existence of a kind of "collective soul", not only for monkeys but for all kinds of beings.

It says that the individual progress of each monkey adds to the progress of this collective soul and directly influences it. When this contribution reaches a certain critical mass, it ends up disseminating that acquisition to the other members and thus evolves the whole species. The reason I am talking about this critical mass issue is very simple: we must try to contribute so that the critical mass of human beings is achieved and thus ensure that everything that is reserved for us takes place as soon as possible.

Depending on what happens, sooner or later, depending on when this critical mass is reached, I believe that we will all have the chance to change our attitudes and stop the process of destruction of the planet's natural resources, and much more. At the moment that each human being improves himself or herself, it will be contributing for the human species to improve as a whole, after all when this critical mass reaches a certain point, we will all "walk faster".

In this sense, there already seems to be a certain critical mass among those who are living, close to the point of being able to understand the cosmic reintegration process, without rebelling. It's as if our spirits were already more or less conscious about the end of the isolation, although we have lived for so long without having open contacts, officially accepted, with beings from other civilizations, that our earthly ego cannot believe it until it happens and catches everyone off guard, unprepared.

We need to unite and seize the opportunity to make progress in all fields, especially in the scientific field, since the scientists will stop calling crazy the ones who try to talk about these issues now.

There will still be many problems… We are not the ones who created most of them, but we will suffer the consequences if we decide not to do anything about them.

It is expected, at least on my part, that a "wave of awareness" will take place that will involve us and help us to foster development in the various fields of science and, above all, in ethics, linked to the laws of the Universe. Now, let's get back to Jan Val Ellam's explanations and let's go a little deeper.

As we said at the end of the second chapter and mentioned again near the end of the third chapter, according to Jan Val Ellam, the Talm Project aimed to migrate the life from "brahmaloka" to "buhloka".

Until the Talm Project, there existed Brahma, Shiva and Vishnu, and their clones and demons. There was no life in the "buhloka".

They decided to create a being, let's call it Mohen So, who had 4 heads being one of Brahma, one of Shiva, one of Vishnu and an independent one, so that this being could analyze the creation and feel the dramas and anxieties that all the 3 felt and with its independent head of control and mental sealing of the 3, he was expected to produce a "strategy of salvation," not only for the 3 of them, but for all who inhabited the "brahmaloka".

NIDANA was the first type of DNA agreed between these beings that arose in the "brahmaloka", which should be worked in the "buhloka" for life to arise there.

This code was the genetic sum of their 3 codes, because they also wanted to feel like the owners of the kind of life that would appear in the "buhloka".

Since none of the races of clones and demons were able to put it into practice and develop the agreed strategy, they created another category of beings to serve as guinea pigs. Let's call them FENVANS.

The FENVANS were created weaker than the clones and demons to be easily destroyed since they would serve as guinea pigs and something could go wrong. Several generations of FENVANS with the NIDANA base code were created and destroyed. Some others died. For the first time in the "brahmaloka", someone was dying.

After many attempts, since the 3 could never come to full agreement, the final version of NIDANA that would be sent to the "buhloka" was approved and it contained much more the code of Brahma and the clones than the codes of Shiva and Vishnu and the demons. Brahma felt that it would be easier for him to control the "buhloka" type of life.

Each of the 3 built its replicator furnace to carry on with the attempts of artificial insemination in the "buhloka".

The problem is that Brahma was different from Shiva and Vishnu because his spirit has fainted in the **superior spirituality** while those of Shiva and Vishnu can simultaneously act in more than one personification within the creation.

Strangely enough, the spirits of the FENVANS who were destroyed or simply died were just those who occupied the bodies of the first beings that appeared in the "buhloka" (based on the NIDANA that was mostly based on the code of Brahma).

Then, at the beginning of life in the "buhloka", two families emerged (let's call them AYA and AYE) and Mohen So was able to create a personification from himself, which became known as Sophia.

With the passage of millions of years, Sophia has been modifying its NIDANA and managed to create what we call biological life in the "buhloka".

Today, after about 7,7 billion years of the beginning of the Talm Project, homo sapiens DNA is the best version of NIDANA that exists in the universe, and also the latest one. As mankind developed, it was also producing different types of NIDANA that are only found here.

So, according to Jan Val Ellam, almost 6 billions of years separate us from the AYA and AYE, and almost 6 billions of years separate us from Sophia! The Bible describes angels as powerful spiritual beings whom God created to perform specific jobs both in heaven and on Earth. And although the Bible often mentions a "host" of angels, it only names a few. Gabriel, Micael and Raphael are all members of this family called AYA.

During all those billions of years many extraterrestrial civilizations were generated in the "buhloka". NIDANA has always been changing and remodeling up to a point where what we call sexuality came up. This has made possible for any individual to be able to create a new individual, simply from the sexual contest of the biological nature of each world.

Almost any man and woman can have sex and have a child or more. No demon or clone has ever been born like us. They emerged in their cocoons, laboratories or wherever it may be, but they were never the fruit of a sexual relationship that resulted in a birth.

During the last 8 billion years, the innumerable generations of "brahmaloka" beings have turned their attention to what happens in the "buhloka".

And what is reserved for us?

Operational spirituality attempt is to make, in the future, less corrupt spirits occupy the bodies based on the NIDANA of homo sapiens… that is what is reserved for us!

For now, let's focus on understanding that Jesus was born on Earth and that this was programmed by Sophia with the assistance of the family AYA and AYE. Although we are referring a lot to Brahma, Shiva and Vishnu, it is the demons and clones (also called angels) that always act in the operational processes and truly control the experiences.

Throughout the creation of the homo sapiens, diverse races of so-called extraterrestrial beings were present on Earth. Also, the interuniversal portals were open. Many of the Gods of the past are demons of "brahmaloka". Some others are Gods but their origin is the "buhloka".

Think of all the names of Gods of the ancient cultures... Namely: Odin, Thor, Chronos, Zeus, Apollo, Lucifer, Enki, Enlil, Krishna, Ganesha, Quetzalcoatl and so on, they all fall into one of these cases. Some are "portal beings" of "brahmaloka", others were created in the "buhloka" and they move in ships and artificial worlds by our physical universe. All of them exist or existed!

Shiva and Vishnu often used the bodies from one of these families and created Avatars of themselves. Brahma, as he can not do this, acts by trying to control everyone that was created from his NIDANA. He uses his clones and tries to make pacts with certain beings, including homo sapiens.

During the 8 billion years in which the Talm Project has been evolving the NIDANA and creating different possibilities around the "buhloka", a lot of problems emerged and needed to be handled by Sophia and his assistants – clones and demons.

Brahma did not trust in Shiva at all, but he trusted in Vishnu a little, so sometimes, due to his incapabilities of controlling a certain situation, he would allow Vishnu to do something.

The problem was that Brahma controlled the clones and often tried to control the demons as well. Shiva and Vishnu were able to maintain control of certain demons, but the disputes never stopped existing.

What we call Lucifer's rebellion has completely changed the course of things in the "buhloka" and started in Capella system about 700,000 years ago, which is about 500,000 years before homo sapiens began to exist.

We should not think that Lucifer is evil and that all beings who have joined the so-called "Lucifer's Rebellion" are also evil or became evil because they have joined the rebellion... This is another distortion of religious conditioning!

This concept of good or evil, within a universe that has been created and managed in a problematic way, covers different levels of meaning. To be evil, the subject must be able to choose between good and evil, which was not and is not the case of most clones and demons and the species that came later on. Let's call these species "bio-demons", since they are races of transition between the NIDANA of the FENVANS and the biological beings that emerged only recently in the "buhloka".

Lucifer belonged to one of the many bio-demons families who performed specific tasks in distant worlds, long before homo sapiens appeared on this planet.

He or she, since Lucifer possessed no sexual gender, was regarded as a being of considerable wit and knowledge. At that time, the newly created bio-demons families had the most modern NIDANA of the "buhloka" and with greater chances of mental freedom to break certain seals and to perceive innumerable philosophical questions that for most beings of that time were unthinkable and unattainable.

This rebellion was not the first that appeared in the "buhloka" but it was the most serious because it infected a very large number of beings, from various families and that inhabited and circulated through different worlds.

We do not want to get into the details, because we only have poor metaphors based on human language to describe events. However, let's focus on what is most important to be understood about rebellion and its consequences.

In the first place, let's understand that over these eight billions of years, the emerging beings did not possess what we might call the awakened philosophical critical sense, and what today seems simple for a human being to ask and understand was, and still is, unreachable for many of these beings, especially the older ones.

Lucifer's problem was precisely having realized that this universe is imperfect, sick, unjust and cruel in terms of nature. This perception modified Lucifer's NIDANA and he was not prepared for it. No one was, even because these beings had interconnected circuits and his mutation was impossible to disguise.

The clones that help and advise Sophia are the same under the control of Brahma. What Lucifer perceived was already perceived just by a few, but no one could provide further explanations to appease Lucifer's mind.

When Lucifer fell unhealthy, it was as if some kind of virus had infected many beings at the same time and no one knew how to deal with that unusual situation.

We should not think that Brahma can always maintain the same performance of control over everything and everyone. During the uprising of the rebellion, for example, he was in a state we call depressive and therefore, Sophia addressed the worlds in which the rebellion was strengthening to try to manage the problem.

Lucifer and several other beings began to become more critical of the universe's management plan, but they still had respect for higher authorities like Sophia. It was only with time that this reverence came to be associated with ignorance.

None of the superior authorities who until then were revered admitted that the universal creator was an unhealthy and needy being. None of them could break the seals of their NIDANA. Sophia could do very little to contain the rebellion, even because the creator himself was a being absent from the buhloka.

After many attempts to contain the uncontrolled mind of the rebel beings, it was defined and accepted by all that the system of worlds under the influence of Lucifer and his ideals should be administered by the rebels themselves and should be isolated from cosmic coexistence with other systems of worlds.

And so it was done. Several worlds in the same system of rebellious governance were isolated to evolve among themselves.

By this time, on planet Earth, Brahma clones had already sown the NIDANA molecule that made life spring, but it was still developing in an irrational way and the homo sapiens still did not even exist. The rebellion occurred in our galaxy but in other star systems, starting in Capella system, as we have said.

Since the rebels did not have enough power to self-manage, the existential pattern in the isolated worlds has been declining. Problems of all kinds began to arise and the rebels were not ready. Many of the beings that were part of the rebellion began to regret having joined and required that the old administrators regain control.

When more than half the population of one world chose to re-belong to the circuits that were not isolated, the other part was removed to some other world yet rebellious, and that planet belonged again to the administration of Sophia and her assistants.

The Nephilim of the bible appeared in some of these worlds as a product of the rebellion and sometime later, as they were without options, they ended up coming to Earth. But they were not the only outsiders who wanted to own the Earth.

For what we now call our planet, various races of beings converged, including clones, demons, bio-demons and biologicals. Most came in their ships, and another part probably came through portals of the "brahmaloka". The confusion was great and no one understood this whole context that is now beginning to be described.

7

WHO IS PREPARED FOR TOMORROW

"Good sense is of all things in the world the most equally distributed, for everybody thinks himself so abundantly provided with it, that even those most difficult to please in all other matters do not commonly desire more of it than they already possess. It is unlikely that this is an error on their part; it seems rather to be evidence in support of the view that the power of forming a good judgment and of distinguishing the true from the false, which is properly speaking what is called Good sense or Reason, is by nature equal in all men. Hence too it will show that the diversity of our opinions does not proceed from some men being more rational than others, but solely from the fact that our thoughts pass through diverse channels and the same objects are not considered by all. To be possessed of good mental powers is not sufficient; the principal matter is to apply them well".

René Descartes[1]

No matter what religion we follow - it does not even matter if we have a religion, as it has already been said - the leadership aspect of a being like Jesus is undeniable for all of us. The visit of the extraterrestrials we are about to receive will make us realize how small we are before the cosmos.

I wonder what will happen to the earthly "religious" when Jesus fulfills his promise to return to "separate the tares from the wheat"...

This time, no longer being born as a man, as it happened two thousand years ago, but rather by visiting us as a kind of "cosmic authority". Jan Val Ellam says this cosmic authority needs us very much. He needs us to help fix this creation and also help fix the creator. And we do that by evolving, spiritually speaking, but that is another story.

If we had the chance to receive Jesus back here on this planet, his life would probably be at risk again, for it would again be considered a threat to power.

Possibly, the believers of the religions that formed based on him and

his teachings would find themselves better than the rest of humanity...

Everyone would probably wait for him to use his powers to solve the

problems here, just as it was done by some apostles and followers, in the time when he was alive on our planet ...

However, it seems to me that this will not be the case this time! He will come not only because humans need it, but it seems to me the universe needs it to happen!

I know it sounds crazy, but after analyzing what seems to have been the promise that Jesus repeated the most while alive, and that miraculously managed to survive the "file burning" of our earthly past, I can't help but consider he will indeed come.

This time, no longer being born on Earth, but coming from outside, probably in a giant ship, in a way that we can all perceive him, as well as the other members of his team, overcoming physical limitations that could inhibit the expression of love, or so I imagine it will be.

After all, no one knows for sure how this moment will be or how long it will last, but we know - or at least judge from what can be read in the Apocalypse and other books - that it is already very close and that major modifications in the world should be done, hopefully for the better, depending on our free will.

Despite the existence of all these beings, our success seems to depend largely on ourselves, which is troubling.

Just quoting some of the "file burnings" I mentioned at the beginning of this chapter, in order to better illustrate what we mean by this term, we have Nabon-Assar, king of Babylon, who in the year 747 BC ordered that all the bronze screens be broken, that all the libraries should be burned, and that everything from the age before his reign should be destroyed, for he wanted to be the first king of the world's history.

In 213 BC, Chin-Chi-Hoang-Ti burned all the Chinese empire's libraries with news of 25 centuries. The destruction of Jerusalem, by the Romans in AD 70, spared no documents. Finally, let us remember that when the library of Alexandria was destroyed at the time of Julius Caesar, it is estimated that about 700,000 ancient greek volumes were lost.

It is not the intention of this author to massage no one's egos, nor to denigrate any religion whatsoever. Simply - after all, I have this right - I ask: what will happen if Jesus, or Sophia, really comes to pay us a visit here on Earth, still in the time of this life we have now? Who convinces me that this is impossible? I know many people who read Jan Val Ellam's books and are also convinced he is coming...

If so, how will things come to be in this world? How will religions be transformed? How long will his presence last? And the extraterrestrials who assist him? How will the world see these things at the moment they are occurring? All I can do is wait and prepare myself to see it with my own eyes.

A friend once made a comment that caught my attention. He said that if this were to happen the world would be a little boring because everyone would be "good".

I do not believe that if it happens everyone will just turn into "good" in the blink of eye... But, it's incredible, isn't it? The human race has reached such a level that it can't even imagine a better way of life than what we have in our world, which is not coincidentally the only thing our physical brain knows. I asked him how he imagined heaven would be like, and he told me that he can only imagine a dull heaven too, only with angels playing harps in the clouds, without much to do.

But returning to the subject of **Jesus' Return**[2] - or as it is said in the Apocalypse of the Bible, the moment of the seventh trumpet's blown - this intervention of Jesus/Sophia is perhaps the only way, capable of provoking a revolution within each one of us.

That's what we need to change on the planet: the way we see the big picture and ourselves!

We need to make such an intimate and individual revolution that, without it, no political system will ever succeed. Without this revolution made quietly within our souls and the elegance of our postures before life, there will be no way out for our planet, nor for ourselves as human beings and, spiritually speaking, as eternal beings.

Adam and Eve were not the first homo sapiens to be created. The story that exists in the Bible is actually an imprecise reproduction of some of the facts.

Around 250,000 years ago, there were only humanoid species without awakened rationality living on the planet as a result of the development of the NIDANA that was planted billions of years before. And it would be exactly on this species that **superior spirituality** would make use of the most strategic stage of its purpose of creating the "philosophical reason" connected to "freedom of thought", among the beings of the universe.

Several races performed scientific experiments on the humanoids until a specimen could be named what today we call homo sapiens.

The real intention of the beings who made these experiences

was not necessarily to create a species that had intelligence and mental freedom to evolve. It was simply to test, get knowledge, and maybe, who knows, to create a species that could obey commands and perform some type of work. We, modern humans, do that to this day performing experiences with the animals of our planet.

When the species homo sapiens arose, Sophia realized how different it was in terms of potentials compared to the other races that contained previous kinds of NIDANA. He realized the importance of the emergence of this new type of NIDANA and many other beings realized the same.

There were not few who tried to dominate the newest species generated in the "buhloka" and around 17 isolated groups of homo sapiens came to be raised, like cattle.

What was happening on Earth was the focus of attention of a whole spiritual government that acts despite all the difficulties in this problematic universe. It was also the focus of the "brahmaloka" beings, also the beings who had not rebelled in the "buhloka" and also the beings that still remained of the rebellion.

When Brahma succeeded in surviving the depression, he began to analyze how Sophia had administered Lucifer's rebellion and was following up on its developments, including the emergence of homo sapiens.

About 20 thousand years ago, Brahma chose an Adam (male) and then an Eve (female) and isolated them in an environment known as the Garden of Eden. This couple was isolated from the conviviality with other homo sapiens, as well as from the domination of other races. He and his clones protected this couple in the Garden of Eden, in order to bring forth a lineage that would trust and reverence Brahma. Oe at least, that was the plan.

Brahma planned to isolate this couple and from it generate a descendant of beings that obeyed him and that he could control, just as he tried to do with the clones and demons.

Those two were admonished, disciplined, influenced, and oriented on many issues. I must affirm that Brahma devoted himself to educating, in his own way, that couple that for him would be the civilizing focus from which an entire species could then derive. But he always demanded blind obedience to his designs, for it is his nature to act with that disposition.

In time, the "Eve" of history, openly resolved not to obey all the instructions or orders of the Creator. She also influenced her partner to act in the same way. Eve was under the influence of many beings, such as the Olympians and Titans, and one of the daughters of Zeus, known as Pandora.

Always "a step behind" from the attitude of Eve regarding the repudiation of the domination of Brahma and his clones, the biblical Adam, sometime later, by the weight of the violent pressure imposed, created a psychological trait of feeling "wrong" towards the creator. The expulsion that the couple would suffer from that privileged area in terms of water and plenty of food, further affected his mind, tired of so much cowardice of powerful beings that tortured, without being aware of it, the fragile humans of those days. This "first human of that generation," by the profound brainwashing that was imposed upon him, became the "first to be found indebted to the creator."

When Brahma, in the bible known as Yahweh, commands Abraham to kill his firstborn son, this was nothing more than an attempt to control humans. It is an attempt to build a submissive NIDANA. The moment Abraham decides to kill his own son in obedience to Brahma, he transforms his NIDANA. Brahma did this to everyone, beginning with Adam himself.

Sometime later, Jesus would arise, pointing to himself as the only one capable of establishing, clarifying, or restoring the harmony between Brahma and his earthly creatures, lost since an "Eve" unsubordinated herself. For more details on that, one can read "O Sorriso de Pandora" (The Pandora's Smile) by Jan Val Ellam.

When Brahma realized that he had lost control of Adam and Eve, he became annoyed and decided to plot a new strategy of domination.

Brahma also realized that Shiva and Vishnu were creating avatars of themselves to act on the planet and since he could not do the same, he decided to choose certain humans and began to make pacts with these humans through their clones to dominate them through what we can call religion, or in other words, mind control.

Brahma made deals with most descendants described in the Bible that arose from Adam and Eve. Seeing that it was very difficult to achieve his goals simply through these pacts, to improve his chances he decided to determine that all races of beings other than the homo sapiens should go away from Earth. Those who did not obey his command were expelled, imprisoned or destroyed.

The fact is that the newest universal race caused curiosity, enchantment, strangeness, and ambition in many of the planetary races scattered throughout the cosmos. In short, the humans of the Earth attracted, without being aware or responsible, a countless avalanche of problems that, if it were not for the decision to isolate them from the cosmic coexistence, the evolution of the species would be compromised. There is also the other side of the coin, that is, the problems arising from isolation.

Anyway, the isolation is about to be officially revoked. It is only a matter of time and at any moment the whole planet will witness the beginning of the cosmic reintegration of the Earth.

8

THE ENOCH AND JESUS SOLUTION

As we mentioned in the end of chapter 7, Brahma had to change his strategy. Now the "Lila" dispute was centered on the descendants of Adam and Eve.

When Enoch arose, Brahma and his clones identified that Enoch was a reincarnation of the same spirit that in the past was in one of the members of the Val family, one of the most recent bio-demons families who had perished and who had now reincarnated.

Since Brahma could not have avatars of his own, he decided to make a pact with Enoch and tried to implement a new strategy to regain control of humanity.

Enoch was visited by clones who informed him that he had been chosen by Brahma to leave Earth and live with these beings and sign a covenant to represent Brahma before humans. Enoch spent 300 years out of Earth and when he returned he produced more than 360 books.

These books have unfortunately been destroyed and only fragments of 2 of these books have survived to this day. Later, Enoch was again taken to the brahmaloka and did not die on

Earth. But the problem is that Enoch eventually passed away out of Earth and Brahma had now lost his chosen one.

Is it not strange that a "god" must make covenants at all times? Brahma tried to make pacts with several people! After Enoch, it was Noah's turn. It was the only thing he could do.

Noah was told that there would be a great flood on the planet and that only his family would live, and that from the descendants of Noah he would be able to do what he had already tried to do from Adam.

There really was the flood but many other genetic lineages survived. Brahma's plans and pacts never worked out completely.

Summing up, Brahma jumps from chosen to chosen and ends up in Abraham and later in Jacob. Jacob, after signing the pact with Brahma, changed his name to Israel. His 12 sons became the progenitors of the "Tribes of Israel".

Since the covenants were not having the expected effect, Vishnu decides to offer another alternative. He, Vishnu, would become man and be born among the descendants of Jacob and would rescue humanity for the control of Brahma.

As Brahma relied more on Vishnu than on Shiva, and seeing no other alternative, he ended up accepting Vishnu's terms. Then, using the NIDANA of Sophia, the clones managed to perform an artificial insemination in Mary and Jesus was born on the planet.

Brahma's expectation was that the human form produced through Sophia would come into the world to fulfill the desires of Brahma. This happened several generations after the famous pact of the 10 commandments, as we all know.

Brahma expected that Jesus would become the emperor of the Jewish people and of the intire planet Earth, but Jesus did not use his "superpowers" to dominate anyone. He, when beaten, offered the other cheek, did not react, and said that his kingdom was not of this world.

The human being Jesus was the best version of a being for the spirit who personified Vishnu, Mohen So and Sophia, among others. As we have said, unlike the most of us, his spirit manages to support more than one being simultaneously in this creation.

He tried to teach mankind to do good and to love unconditionally. Brahma, in not having his expectations met felt betrayed and that is why Jesus was crucified. And the funny thing is that humanity thinks that "God" sent his son to die for us and save us from our sins. This is another absurd religious distortion.

Honestly, it is obvious that Jesus was born on this planet so that his spirit could "communicate" with a whole plurality of generations of beings, and especially with Brahma.

Anyone who can understand this will build quite interesting neural paths for the next mental constructions around this disturbing subject. Jan Val Ellam has been trying to reproduce this complex context as he thinks it can or should be done. Unfortunately, only the general context of the lectures and books he has been able to publish somewhat gives an adult view and close to the "truth".

Why did not Jesus address this problem at the time of his life? Either his human condition was deceived by Brahma and his clones and he only discovered it in the last days of his earthly life or he chose to leave it for another time. However, something seems to have occurred shortly after his crucifixion, which led him to act, revealing some of these issues which were considered as Gnostic.

We are led to think that it was still the same Jesus, with his human nature, acting as resurrected, but it was not, since Sophia has been the protagonist since the death of Jesus. Jesus, as a human, made promises about "his return", which will be fulfilled, not by someone with his human nature, but by a being who has nothing of human and who has been trying to assimilate in his NIDANA the characteristics of humans.

9

POLICIES OF NATIONS

"Are not we an organized fantasy? An incoherence that works and a disorder that acts?" **Paul Valéry**[1]

Sometimes I try to observe the world to understand what is going on, but all I can perceive are scattered parts of a family that despite living in the same planetary residence, does not see each other as a whole.

Seeing wars, conflicts, religious disputes by believers, deceit, lies, disease, disregard for life, atomic and nuclear weapons, arms race, state terrorism, I wonder how this world can work without self-destructing.

I wonder how we manage to move on, with so much dishonesty, intrigues and uncontested interests disputing space. Honesty and ethics seem to have almost been swept away from the planet, and only in classical literature and old films we can find its remnants.

What amazes me is that after World War II it has been demonstrated that airpower is of extreme importance if you are planning to win a war. So, it seems logical to conclude that all nations have made their efforts not to ignore anything unusual in their skies. I am pretty sure that all nations know that UFOs are a common thing and they all have their "secret reports".

So, isn't it more intelligent to create policies that should be considered a guide on how to act regarding UFO phenomenon? Wouldn't it be more intelligent to start preparing the world for an eventual official contact? I am sure the Vatican also knows that UFOs and Aliens are real, why don't they talk about it?

Clearly, no one talks about it because they don't understand the Big Picture! They don't know what to say!

If we became aware of the "sickness" of the creator, as Jan Val Ellam presents, established in our DNA, and also all the extraphysical influence that mankind has received, we would see clearly why the nations of Earth live in constant discord.

There is no policy in place that dignifies life and gives us reasonable hope for the future.

In addition, we can say that another great cause of discord among participants in a group is the ignorance, ignorance, of the rules of the "game of existence".

The ordinary people do not know, at least while I write these pages, whether spirits exist or not, whether aliens exist, or if each one is actually given accordingly to one's works...

Why do we not even know if there is life after death?

It all leads back to the problem of this creation and its creator...

The situation is so hard to deal with that only through humans, **superior spirituality** seems to have found a way to start explaining what is went wrong in this creation! The ability that certain humans have of seeing spirits is kind of unique in this universe, according to Jan Val Ellam...

So, as soon as we all have a better view of the Big Picture it is crucial that we take a step forward and try to change things for the better.

But, officially, the only thing we "know" is what "science" can prove. And that is why certain facts will need to occur so that all our concepts and values take on another dimension.

The great wave of awareness, the fuel necessary to promote a reformation in the "way of accomplishing things here on Earth" is a step that, possibly, will only be a reality in the day in which there is an intervention of some celestial authority and that will modify the way of thinking and acting of the majority of souls linked to our planet.

Recently, I watched a film about the life of Giordano Bruno who was criminally burned alive as a heretic because he naively hoped that the power-owners - the elite of the Roman curia associated with the Dodge and the rulers of Venice - would reform their power. "Sancta Simplicitas," as **Jerome of Prague**[2] would say, who was also burned alive as a heretic, for supporting the ideals of his friend Jan Huss, another whose life was also taken away by the fire promoted by the owners of power, about two centuries before Giordano Bruno.

Jesus was someone who endeavored to awaken in the masters of power at that time, the higher faculties of the human being so that he could reform himself and then improve the world around him. Except he was not naive, for he knew what to expect. Nevertheless, he preferred to lose his life to disfigure his personal code of conduct, a mark of his heavenly personality which, it seems, will soon be better known. But that's Jesus. And we, how will we act?

Are we going to repeat the revolutions that destroy and never get anywhere, or do we use all the creativity daring to inspire ourselves in the legacy they have left us, even if we are not close to thinking like Gandhi or Jesus?

According to Jan Val Ellam, the human DNA is very precious for this universe's creator! It is precious for Brahma, Shiva and Vishnu (Trimurti)! It is precious for Sophia!

We are capable of loving and we have great reasoning freedom, and that is precious for the universe! We are far from being perfect beings, as we all know, we need to evolve, spiritually speaking, but our body is "the best body available" in terms of DNA possibilities in this universe. We live in a pretty decent planet too, in cosmic terms.

All of this is the "scenario" in which many other beings would like to be living in...

All governments should unite and make sure that every nation on Earth is prosper. The fact that there is almost no policy in place in the sense of bringing us together as earthily citizens makes it really hard for any extraterrestrial being to come here!

If a cosmic authority wishes to pay us a visit, where would he land? In the USA? Why? Why not in Brazil? Why not in Russia? Why not in Jerusalem? Why not at the Vatican? I could go on and on...

I believe this first official contact will be very fast and not very deep, in terms of information exchanging, because the only way this can ever work is if it is conducted in homeopathic doses. We need to see ourselves as brothers and partners of an existential adventure and, so far, we have not succeed in doing that even among us, human beings who live together in a single planet.

10

HERE IS THE ANSWER

"I write because I have the impression or the feeling that the world is unfinished, as if God, who created the world in six days and rested in the seventh, had not had time to do everything."
Antonine Maillet[1]

"Generalizing I think that every human being, in his sphere of activity, small or large, can be an artisan of the eighth day."
Hubert Reeves[2]

It is a fact that, for the first time in human history, mankind has the means to self-destruct. Life on the planet is complicated. But for the first time we will stop being ignorant about being alone in the universe, which can lead to deep understandings about existence itself. There is nothing left but to believe and work in the sense that it is perfectly possible for an evolved civilization to attain higher levels of evolution without self-destruction. It is our only hope!

Now we can see that the industrial model developed by man is inconsequential, since it constitutes the main threat to the survival of our own species, as well as the main threat to the planet as a whole.

This industrial model is globally embedded within a capitalist system and a "system of religious beliefs" that has allowed us to increase social inequality, the destruction of the environment and the alienation of almost everyone on the planet.

It would not be unwise to even believe that a destructive process similar to that which is going on on Earth may already have occurred in other worlds, possibly in other times. We must therefore consider the hypothesis that instead of "conquerors, dominators and explorers of worlds" some evolved aliens are "saviors of worlds and spirits".

We just do not know where all this is going to go, so it's important to start thinking globally. The changes of nature are already there, the tsunamis and hurricanes and, moreover, the fall of the towers of the World Trade Center followed by the wars of Afghanistan and Iraq which, again according to the aforementioned book The Seventh Trumpet of the Apocalypse: The Return of Jesus, of Jan Val Ellam, precede the return of Jesus/Sophia, have already occurred and other "disasters" should come.

The new century must be that of knowledge and spiritualization linked to the creation of an ideal of planetary citizenship, otherwise we will all be on the way to the end of the planet.

Of the two, one: either the new generations and the authorities of the world attempt to this perspective or perhaps the human race ceases to exist in some centuries, which is a very serious problem for spirits who, in our example, do not have options of merit for incarnate in other less primitive transitory worlds.

In addition to this question, understanding the context invisible to our eyes enables us to pass through the temporary experience (or transitory if you prefer), which is to live on Earth or in other transitory worlds in a happier and calmer way, without so much to revolt with God, to natural disasters, to the mistakes of our neighbors, and to analyze ourselves with our own mistakes. This is because, as we immerse ourselves in the study of the spiritual background that surrounds the earthly life, we begin to perceive the existence of laws of cause and effect, which forces us to seek constant personal improvement, guarding our own attitudes, which , let's face it, is already a gain in personal progress. Thus, we improve ourselves and the world we live in.

I would like to emphasize that it is also in this material life that we need to focus and, so that it doesn't continue to be a "torture", we need to embellish the planet urgently with our small daily attitudes, each within its sphere of action and according to its conscience, as quickly as possible.

So we can try to understand a little the strategy of beings who love us and who want our evolution from other planes that we can not glimpse while we are "alive", and who have been donating to it for a good few years.

To live life worthily, we don't even have to believe in God or try to understand Him. It suffices that we understand a little about the laws of the universe and the invisible laws of existence, which more evolved spirits tried to show us, giving their testimony while they were incarnated here. To love unconditionally seems only to be the first step to understanding them.

In the end, it seems to me more logical to conclude that such an incredible work - as I humbly characterize the great work of existence and the universe in itself, considering all the spiritual context and not only the material - has been created by some kind of intelligence that I, influenced by the culture of the world in which I was born, usually give the name of God, and not the result of chance, as the most skeptical believe. I try not to confuse this God with any other being.

The mere idea of the existence of a greater and unknown

force of which we are all part, being potential gods or dormant gods, since we are eternal and have the capacity to think, seems comfortable enough for me to go on believing in God, trying to love to be loved, even with all the defects we have. This is already one of the beauties of diversity and of life itself.

We must find the formula to love life and accept it with its difficulties trying to overcome its limitations in search of evolution, being eternal discontented, but without ever revolting or wishing to have another life, or simply waiting for a better future, financially, and contributing little, either after death or "here on this side" so that things really change.

Believe it: our spirits are eternal! I say "eternal discontents" so that we never become insensitive to suffering. Of the nonconformists, perhaps it was Martin Luther King (1929-1968) - an American pastor who exposed himself in the fight against racism and died murdered - who best translated this feeling, because when asked if his attitude would really serve for something, used to say:

> *It is better to try and fail than to see life go by.*
> *It is better to try, still in vain, than to sit doing nothing until*
> *   the end.*
> *I prefer in the rain to walk that in sad days at home to hide me.*
> *I prefer to be happy, although crazy, who accordingly live.*

What should be done anyway? The answer is simple. Modifying how we think, how we educate our children, how teachers educate their students, how entrepreneurs work in their businesses, how politicians work after being elected, how religious leaders manipulate consciences, how we poison our physical body and our spirit through bad habits and bad thoughts, how we treat our neighbor and our servants, anyway...

We need to change practically everything, relearning that it is not bullshit to love existence and respect nature. Easy, isn't it? Whether it's easy or not, it needs to be done!

By nature, we are monkeys with spirits of "potential gods" asleep during life.

Our science already knows that there is only a 1.6 percent difference between our DNA and chimpanzee DNA.

Now it is time to help unravel the second part of our nature, which is that of sleeping gods – and for that, perhaps, what most of us understand as science is still not enough!

I confess that sometimes I find it hard to say what science already knows and what it does not yet know, but I know that most scientists in the world do not believe in spirits and do not admit the existence of other humanities because they failed to prove their existence "scientifically speaking".

What seems to differentiate us from the rest of the animals that exist on Earth does not seem to be the ability to think and speak, science advances in the sense of clarifying through experiences with many animals that this they can also do, at different levels, according to their species.

What sets us apart is the nature of our spirits, from the accumulated experiences we have had throughout our lives, and science fails to delve deeper into this aspect.

To finish, no matter how hard we work, to formulate ideal systems of living in society, we know, deep down in our souls, that our planet will have no future if we do not design it to be ecologically sustainable. Thankfully, many people around the world are already looking at this issue, and trying to change the environment around them within the parameters of sustainability, regardless of what they believe in.

I humbly hope that, thanks to more "favors" from Jesus and his team, we will soon have the opportunity to expand this concern for all men and women who live here. But let's not deceive ourselves because it won't be anyone from outside who will do for us what we desperately needs to be done: learn to honor life by living as honest and loving citizens.

The word "favors" is in quotation marks, because what I want to say is that there is a right way to do favors, and surely it is not solving for us the problems we create; but showing us, even at the cost of personal sacrifices like many did, what to do, and how to act to save the world and the universe.

Besides, whoever is really a leader does not do this or that please anyone; they do it out of love, and they are masters of the art of giving and unconditionally loving their neighbor. If we verify the conduct of the great men and women who ennobled our species, true leaders of planetary progress, we may observe that all have acted in this way.

Because they do not know how to act otherwise, and as true leaders they are, they serve those led by love, with the goal that, one day, they latter will be able to develop a code of principles and values that will honor life, finding the formula to architect happiness in their consciences and in the world in which they live.

It is, after all, our turn. Get to work!

As I said, we probably are the most privileged beings in the universe, of brahmaloka and of buhloka!

We will be able to go to **superior spirituality** if we clean ourselves up... And the good news is that we die fast! If, throughout an earthily life, the spirit learns to clean itself and does not acquire karma, it can succeed and achieve, in the course of a lifetime, what a spirit trapped in a long-lived but diseased body can not do in billions of years!

Do we need to be helped? I think so! But in this chaotic universe, who does not need it? But the problem is that the religious distortion ends up conditioning the man to think that a being, Jesus, or whoever, will come from outside to solve our problems and help us to evolve.

We think that if there are other extraterrestrial beings, they must be spiritualized and evolved and will come to Earth to help us solve our problems. Not quite!

Sophia will not come this way, and it is us who need to understand the plan of the superior spirituality and execute it from the inner reformation and the good examples that serve to inspire us to promote the good within creation.

I am one of those who think and work for a new "rebirth" for this humanity, from the unusual facts that the resumption of contact with beings of other realities, and the scientific advance that will inevitably be produced in the human psyche, can happen in the best way for everyone involved.

The pursuit of enlightenment and "truth," not this "rot of weirdnesses" that was "canonized as sacred", is essential to free oneself from the ignorance collected as "truth".

AFTERWORD

"The ideas I stand for are not mine. I borrowed them from Socrates, robbed them of Chesterfield, stole them from Jesus. And if you do not like their ideas, what would be the ideas you would use?"
 Dale Carnegie[1]

It is the intention of this author to spread the belief that, very soon, we must witness a unique moment in our history, which is the reunion with Sophia/Jesus and the beginning of a period of direct contact with other civilizations of the universe.

I called this planet a Fantasy Island due to the fact that we are all living without the perception of a whole larger context that surrounds us. We seem lost in the midst of an infinite universe, not knowing if spirits and extraterrestrials exist, without greater clarifications regarding the meaning of life and our past, and frustrated with the things that occur in our daily life.

In the first two chapters of this book I tried to clarify the spiritual contexto and, in talking about the existence of extraterrestrials, it is not absurd to assume they must also have similar or identical kinds of spirits to that of every human. We would therefore be cosmic brothers using different bodies, according to the aspects of nature and the particular evolution of each inhabited world.

I also tried to demonstrate that it is quite reasonable to believe that other beings have reasons to fear direct contact with the citizens of a planet as unequal and violent as ours.

In the second and third chapters, I also introduced Jan Val Ellam's explanations about the "brahmaloka" and the "buhloka" and talked about the peculiar spiritual question that surrounds us, inhabitants of Earth, since our spirits are still "imprisoned" - in the sense of not possessing merits to incarnate in other better worlds, if there is any - to terrestrial environments, mainly due to the consequences of Lucifer's rebellion. This subject is necessary for the reader to understand that the coming of Jesus to Earth, when he was born here, is linked with issues from this distant past.

In the third chapter, the intention is to awaken the reasoning for the real consequences of a greater and perfect force existence, whom Jesus called the Loving Father, difficult for us to understand through the reading of the sacred books of religions, as it's the case of the Bible.

I, in particular, believe that about two thousand years ago, a great heavenly authority who became known to us by the name of Jesus, decided to submit to all our follies to show us and others, including the creator, that it is possible to live in a "different" way. And I also believe that this being was not lying when he said that there is a Loving Father, perfect and above it all.

In the fourth, I begin the chapter by commenting on the distance that exists between Earth's religions and their imperfections when compared to the doctrine of life shown by evolved spirits born here in an attempt to help us evolve. The intention is to make the reader reflect on whether religion is something that embellishes the world, or is something that divides it.

Still in the fourth chapter, I return to the discussion around the Bible and Genesis more specifically. This subject serves as a basis for the understanding of the following chapter, which speaks of the Sumerians and which is intended to make the reader realize that there is plenty scientific evidence of the interference of aliens in the history of Earth and men.

In the sixth chapter, I try to go a little deeper into Jan Val Ellam's information, which is also essential to understand why Jesus told us two thousand years ago that he would return to our planet in the future.

In the seventh and eighth chapter I directly discuss the hypothesis of the return and the consequences that this would have on our lives and I also continue to bring more of Jan Val Ellam's explanations about biblical issues.

The ninth chapter is very short and intended to draw readers' attention to the importance of having policies that represent this knowledge.

The tenth chapter concludes the book by trying to make my opinion clear about the way we stumble on this planet. It is to emphasize that we all need to take on the responsibility of modifying ourselves so that we can improve the universe we live in.

Rodrigo Freitas

THANKS TO

I dedicate this book to all those who contribute to my personal happiness and to all the "real" teachers I have had throughout life, in school, in courses, in college, and in daily life. To educators who must be essential in any world.

This book is intended to make the reader begin to question what their eyes cannot see, and to warn the new generations in particular about the possibility of the occurrence of certain events that may have the effect of changing reality here on Earth.

Regardless of anything, we will be the future teachers, administrators, lawyers, judges, politicians, doctors, scientists, biologists, police officers, in short, future managers of the nations of the planet.

The challenge is set. May the God within ourselves give us the strength to change world!

Special thanks to my father and my family, João and Fatinha, the Kummer family, Krysamon and Luciana, Marcelo, Atlan group members and IEEA members, for all the support along this journey.

Rodrigo Freitas

NOTES

BRIEF COMMENTARY

1. *Hubert Reeves (1932):* Born in Montreal, PhD in Nuclear Astrophysics. He wrote several works on the history of the universe and on the great ecological challenges, of which the most famous are "A Little More Blue" (Patience dans l'azur), L'heure de s'enivrer, among others, all in the field of scientific dissemination. He also wrote Malicorne - Reflections of an Observer of Nature, where he quotes Antonine Maillet's "Artisan of the eighth day," quoted in the eleventh chapter of this book.

1. THE MANY ABODES OF THE UNIVERSE

1. *Francisco Cândido Xavier (1910 - 2002):* An internationally renowned spirit medium with outstanding performance in the field of material and spiritual well-being, among other attributes that attest to his noble moral condition and example of love. His mediumistic work, with more than four hundred books on various topics, all donated to philanthropic institutions speak for themselves.
2. **Transcommunications:** There are many people who were born with the capacity to see spirits. For those who want to know more about transcommunication, which is the scientific investigation of the phenomenon of voices and images coming from the beyond, I recommend the book Interdimensional Contacts of Sonia Rinaldi.
3. **Allan Kardec (1804 - 1869):** Pseudonym of the French Hippolyte Leon Denizard Revail (1804-1869), which codified the five basic works of the Spiritist Doctrine, also known as Spiritual Revelation.
4. **Final Judgment:** Allan Kardec's commentary in "The Genesis".

   Chapter XVII - Final Judgment

   The reign of goodness being established upon the earth, it is necessary that spirits hardened in evil, and those who would be able to bring trouble to it, should be excluded. God has given them the necessary time for their improvement; but at the moment when this world is to be elevated in the hierarchy of the worlds, by the moral progress of its inhabitants, having reached such a time, this place will be forbidden to those who have not taken advantage of the instructions which they have come to receive; and such prohibition will apply not only to the incarnates as to the disincarnates of such a group. They will be exiled to lower worlds, as before, on Earth, with the components of the Adamic race; at the same time, will be replaced by more advanced Spirits, it is to this separation that Jesus will preside, which is figured by these words of the final judgment: "The good ones will pass to my right and the bad ones to my left."

The doctrine of a final, single, universal judgment, which puts an end to all humanity, repudiates reason in the sense that it would imply God's inactivity during the eternity that preceded the creation of the Earth, and the eternity that will follow its destruction. What is the use of the sun, the moon, and the stars, which, according to the Book of Genesis, are meant to illuminate our world? It is astonishing that a work so immense has been made to last so little time and for the benefit of beings whose greater part would be in advance towards the eternal torments.

Materially, the idea of a single judgment was, to some extent, admissible to those who do not seek the reason of things, as long as one believed that all humanity was concentrated on the Earth, and that everything in the universe was created for its inhabitants: it is inadmissible since it has become known that there are thousands of similar worlds that perpetuate the humanities during eternity, and among which the Earth is an imperceptible point, the least considerable.

By this one fact we see that Jesus was right to say to his disciples: "There are many things that I can not tell you, for you would not understand them", behold, the progress of science is indispensable to a sound interpretation of some of his parables. Certainly the apostles, St. Paul and the first disciples, would have established other dogmas if they had had the astronomical, geological, physical, chemical, physiological, and psychological knowledge we have today. Jesus also delayed the completion of his instructions, and announced that all things should be restored.

Morally, a definitive judgment without appeal is irreconcilable with the infinite goodness of the Creator, whom Jesus unceasingly presents to us as a good Father, who always leaves an open path to repentance, and is ready to extend his arms to the prodigal son. If Jesus had understood the judgment in this sense, he would have denied his own words.

The judgment, by emigration, as defined above, is rational; is founded on the most rigorous justice, since it leaves eternally to the Spirit, its free will; that it is not the privilege of anyone; that an equal latitude is given by God to all His creatures, without exception, to progress; that even the annihilation of a world that would result in the destruction of the body would not cause any interruption to the progressive march of the Spirit. Such is the awareness of the plurality of worlds and the plurality of existences.

According to this interpretation, by means of emigration, the qualification of final judgment is not exact, since the Spirits go through similar purifications with each renewal of the worlds that they inhabit, until they have reached a certain degree of perfection. There isn't a final judgment, but there are general judgments, in all times of partial or total renewal of the population of the worlds, and as a result of them are the great emigrations and immigrations of the Spirits.

2. A BAD START

1. ***Myth of the Hopi Indians:*** They currently live on a reservation in the state of Arizona, USA. Among other enigmatic stories that form their culture, they claim that their ancestors were visited by beings flying in the air, in flying shields, and who had the power to cut and transport large blocks of stones and to build tunnels and underground facilities.

2. ***Fallen Angels:*** Religious doctrine states that the sins of fallen angels start before the beginning of human history. Accordingly, fallen angels became identified with angels who were led by Satan in rebellion against God and equated with demons.

   Further in this book we will analyze what Jan Val Ellam is bringing in terms of explanations for the fallen angels doctrine and its consequences to Earth.

3. **Hitler, Stalin and Mao Tse Tung:** Respectively heads of state of Nazi Germany, Communist Russia and Communist China that in about four decades, according to the latest historical surveys, were responsible for about one hundred and thirty million deaths.

4. **Brahmanda myth:** It is a text in Sanskrit and one of the eighteen great Puranas, a genre of Hindu texts. The text is named after one of the cosmological theories of Hinduism, namely the "cosmic egg" (Brahma-anda). What Jan Val Ellam is bringing is not a reaffirmation of what is already written; it is his own explanations using the Sanskrit terms to facilitate the understanding of the themes.

5. ***Sophia:*** According to Jan Val Ellam, Sophia is an extraterrestrial being whose job is to administer the buhloka, that is, the physical universe in which the planet Earth is inserted. Throughout the next chapters we will speak more about Sophia, known as the Cosmic Christ. Sophia is one of the avatars of Vishnu, whose spirit also personified Jesus, among other beings.

3. AFFECTED REASONING AND COSMIC IGNORANCE

1. ***Friedrich Nietzsche (1844 - 1900):*** German Philosopher. He wrote several texts criticizing religion, morality, contemporary culture, philosophy and science, exhibiting a predilection for metaphor, irony and aphorism.

   His key ideas included criticism of the Apollonian / Dionysian dichotomy, perspectivism, the will to power, the death of God, the Übermensch and eternal return. Its central philosophy is the idea of "affirmation of life," which involves questioning any doctrine that drains an expansive energy, no matter how socially prevalent these ideas might be.

2. **John the Baptist:** The prophet who announced to the world the arrival of Jesus, traditionally known as the forerunner of Jesus.

4. THE ROLE OF RELIGIONS AND ITS SACRED BOOKS

1. *Napoleão Bonaparte (1769 - 1821):* French emperor who revolutionized European history in the early nineteenth century
2. *Sir Richard Francis Burton (1821 - 1890):* English explorer, writer, translator, linguist, geographer, poet, anthropologist, orientalist, scholar, swordsman, secret agent and diplomat.
3. *Jan Hus (1369 - 1415):* Czech writer and rector of the University of Prague (1409), which attracted the enmity of the upper clergy for denouncing its mediocrity and its wealth, besides the power of the Germans over the Czechs, until it was excommunicated in 1412; was arrested in 1414 at the Council Constance; abandoned by his protector who had given him a safe-conduct, Emperor Sigismund of Luxembourg (1368-1437), being burned as a heretic on July 6, 1415.
4. *Giordano Bruno (1548 - 1600)* and Jan Huss *(1369 - 1415)* are just a few examples I have just cited to illustrate some of the crimes that the Catholic Church has committed. There were more than 5,000 deaths ordered by the Holy Inquisition Court, and there had been humiliations, tortures and pains lighter than death, such as the exile that was imposed on the astronomer Kepler (1571-1630), for example, in the days of Protestantism.

   The philosopher, mathematician and astronomer Giordano Bruno is considered the father of modern philosophy. He was born in 1548 in Italy and died at the stake of the Inquisition on February 17, 1600. Before being murdered by the Church, he was imprisoned for eight years, suffering various types of torture, while responding to accusations of immoral conduct, blasphemy and heresy.

   Giordano, even opposing Catholic dogmatics, believed that the universe was infinite, that God is the universal soul that rules harmony in the world and that all material things are manifestations of this infinite principle. That is, it was not even an atheistic rebellion, but a rebellion in favor of freedom of thought and research, in order to unravel the mysteries of the cosmos, yet it was burned alive. Later, at the place of his death, a statue was erected in his honor and in honor of free thought.
5. *Jerome (c. 347 - 420):* The most notable partisan priest of the church of Alexandria. He was invited by Damaso, bishop of Rome, to organize a book that would unify the Catholic creed around the decisions of the church of Rome, whose bishop intended to wield supremacy over the other bishops of other churches. From the work of Jerome came the Bible as we know it today, in its Latin version called the Vulgate.

5. HAS HUMANITY KNOWN ABOUT THE EXISTENCE OF ETS?

1. *Graham Hancock (1950):* Correspondent, in Africa, for *The Economist* and *Sunday Times* newspapers. Author of several bestsellers, among which *Fingerprints of the Gods*

2. *Zecharia Sitchin (1920 - 2010):* holds a degree in Economic History from the University of London and author of books such as The 12° Planet and Revisited Genesis.

    In this work, Genesis Revisited, shows that many of the great scientific discoveries of the last years were already known of the ancient civilizations, thanks to the intervention of extraterrestrial colonizers.

3. *Book of the Dead:* The sacred book of the ancient Egyptians.

4. *Mahabaratha:* The origin of the Mahabaratha is linked to the oral tradition in India, dating back more than five thousand years. It is considered the greatest epic in the world and it means the "great war of the Bharatas" (Hindus). The main theme is the war between Kauravas (amoral and perverse) against the Pandavas (defenders of virtue) belonging to distinct branches of the same family. Its actor is Krishna Dwaipanya Vyasa, a deity.

5. *Popol Vuh:* The sacred book of the ancient Mayans.

6. WHAT IS RESERVED FOR US?

1. *Zoroaster:* At the age of 20, he left home and spent seven years in solitude in a cave on a mountain. He then returned to his people and at the age of 30 received the Divine Revelation, which began with a series of seven visions. He faced every kind of difficulty in converting people to his new religion. In ten years of preaching he had only one believer - his cousin. He was persecuted and harassed by the priests. The princes refused to give him support and protection and imprisoned him because his new message disturbed tradition and caused confusion in the minds of his subjects. At some point Zoroaster succeeds in influencing King Vishtaspa, who has become a fervent follower of his faith. With his support Zoroastrianism became the official religion of the Persian nation.

    The sacred scriptures of Zoroastrianism are called "Zend-Avesta," which means "Comments on the Knowledge." He founded a civilization of essentially agricultural character impregnated with the practical idea of life designed to educate men in a noble belief and sublime morality.

    The Golden Rule of Zoroastrianism: "Act as you would have them do unto you."

2. *Siddhartha Gautama:* Prince who left the reign he would receive by inheritance, to get to know the world. He passed on posterity as "Buddha, the Enlightened One." On his philosophical and doctrinal legacy, Buddhism is today divided into many different strands.

7. WHO IS PREPARED FOR TOMORROW

1. *René Descartes* **(1596 - 1650):** French philosopher who revolutionized human thought. This passage was taken from the book "Discourse on Method", one of his works.

2. **Some quotations from the gospel and Apocalypse about the promised return of Jesus:**

   "Look He is coming with the clouds. Every eye will see him, even those who pierced him", says the Apocalypse.

   "…Then the sign of the Son of Man will appear in heaven, and then all the tribes of the earth will mourn, and they will see the Son of Man coming on the clouds of heaven with power and great glory" (Mat 24, 30 = Mar 13, 26 = Luc 21, 27).

   "For as the lightning goes forth from the east and shines to the west, so shall be the coming of the son of man? (Mat 24,27).

   "Watch therefore, for you know neither the day nor the hour" (Mat 25,13).

9. POLICIES OF NATIONS

1. *Ambroise Paul Toussaint Jules Valéry* *(1871 – 1945):* Was a French poet, essayist, and philosopher. In addition to his poetry and fiction (drama and dialogues), his interests included aphorismson art, history, letters, music, and current events. Valéry was nominated for the Nobel Prize in Literature in 12 different years.

2. **Jerome of Prague (1360 -1416):** Priest and religious reformer who was burned alive as a heretic in 1416. By the time fire was to be lit, already tied to the wooden trunk, an elderly lady helped to harvest sticks to fan the starting fire. Jerome, seeing that simple attitude, simply said: "sancta simplicitas", that is, "holy ignorance."

10. HERE IS THE ANSWER

1. *Antonine Maillet (1929):* Is an Acadian novelist, playwright, and scholar. She was born in Bouctouche, New Brunswick.

2. *Hubert Reeves (1932):* is a French Canadian astrophysicist and popularizer of science. His career has lasted for nearly fifty years. He won many awards for his works including the Albert Einstein Award.

AFTERWORD

1. ***Dale Breckenridge Carnegie (1888 - 1955):*** was an American writer and lecturer, and the developer of famous courses in self-improvement. One of the core ideas in his books is that it is possible to change other people's behavior by changing one's behavior toward them.

BIBLIOGRAPHY

GIBRAN, Khalil Gibran, Jesus The Son Of Man, translated and presented by Mansour Challita, Gibran International Cultural Association.

CAPRA, Fritjof, The Hidden Connections of Science for a Sustainable Life, translated by Marcelo Brandão Cipolla, São Paulo, Editora Cultrix.

LELOUP, Jean-Yves, If My House Gets Fire, I Would Save the Fire, Names of Gods, Interviews with Edmond Blattchen, 2001, translated by Fundação Editora da UNESP, São Paulo: Unesp, 2002.

REEVES, Hubert, The Eighth Day Craftsmen, Names of Gods, Interviews with Edmond Blattchen, 2000, translated by Fundação Editora da UNESP, São Paulo: Unesp, 2002.

SITCHIN, Zecharia, Genesis Revised, translated by Evelyn K. Massaro and Marcília Brito, 7. ed. São Paulo: Best Seller Publisher.

FERREIRA, Aurélio Buarque de Holanda, Mini Aurélio, The Mini Dictionary of the Portuguese language, 4. ed. Rio de Janeiro: Editora Nova Fronteira.

Holy Bible, Pastoral Edition, São Paulo, Paulus Publishing House.

KARDEC, Allan, Book of Spirits, Translation by Guillon Ribeiro, Copyright by Federação Espírita Brasileira, Brasília, 1994.

KARDEC, Allan, The Genesis, conclude

HANCOCK, Graham, The Digital Gods, translation by Ruy Jungmann, 1st edition, São Paulo, Editora Record, 1999.

ELLAM, Jan Val, Cosmic Reintegration, 3rd edition, São Paulo: Zian, 2002.

ELLAM, Jan Val, Carma E Compromisso, 3rd edition, São Paulo: Zian, 2002.

ELLAM, Jan Val, Spiritual Paths, 3rd edition, São Paulo: Zian, 2002.

ELLAM, Jan Val, The Seventh Trumpet of the Apocalypse: The Return of Jesus, 1st edition, São Paulo, Zian, 2005.

ABOUT THE AUTHOR

Rodrigo Freitas was born in Brazil in 1982. In 2006, he has published his first book called "Earth, a true Fantasy Island". A little later, in 2011, he published a second book called "Utopia of the Desperate". Both books are only available in Portuguese and were inspired by the books published by Jan Val Ellam, who writes about spiritualist information, ufology, history, and many other things. This book is an evolved version of "Earth, a true Fantasy Island". The next goal is to translate some of Ellam's books to English and also to develop an adapted version of them for TV.

ABOUT JAN VAL ELLAM

Jan Val Ellam is the pseudonym used by the Brazilian writer Rogério de Almeida Freitas, to write about convergence points between Christianism, Allan Kardec's doctrine, Ufology, Mythology, Cosmic Disclosure, Universalist Spiritualism and Planetary Citizenship, among others.

It provides new information regarding religious themes and political-philosophical issues related to the homo sapiens adaptation to the challenges of the iminent Cosmic Reintegration. This new information is brought to Jan Val Ellam by spirts, but also by extraterrestrial and extraphysical beings.

Cosmic Reintegration marks unprecedented steps both in the terrestrial and also in the cosmic history. It will be the moment when everyone of this planet will start having a clear notion about the existence of extraterrestrial life, reincarnation, cosmic laws of Ethics and beings like Krishna, Jesus, avatars and Gods from an ancient past.

Until the year 2018, Jan Val Ellam has published more than 30 books and he says he has at least another hundred that he intends to publish before he dies. He alsos gives lectures about these issues on a virtual institute called IEEA – Instituto de Estudos Estratégicos e Alternativos.

Until 2018, he had posted about 200 hundred different lectures, each one with an **average** of 4 hours, available at IEEA. Unfortunately, most of his work is only available in portuguese until now.

In 2018, he has done a lecture in Miami in English, and it is available on **youtube**.

https://youtu.be/MEJ9mv0n5cg

BOOKS PUBLISHED BETWEEN 1996 AND 2000

The central theme of the ideas transmitted at the time by the mentors was the end of the cosmic isolation of the Earth, with the consequent resumption of the cosmic exchange with extraterrestrial civilizations, which would have as a historical and political landmark the return of the Master Jesus, in his cosmic body.

The trilogy "Fall and Spiritual Ascension".
Book 1) Cosmic Reintegration.
Book 2) Spiritual Paths.
Book 3) Karma and Commitment.

This trilogy also introduced a superficial approach to Lucifer's rebellion - later he would publish a deeper one - placed in the context of several capelin biodemic families exiled to Earth, as the product of the Luciferian problem.

Other themes of the trilogy: (1) the relationship between Jesus and Lucifer; (2) the fall of the angels and the roles of Lucifer and Satan; (3) the extraterrestrial and spiritual panels involving life on Earth; (4) the connection of the unfolding of Lucifer's rebellion with the formation of earthly humanity; (5) reincarnation as the basic process of cosmic continuity; (6) The human context to the cosmic question; among others.

Far Beyond the Horizon. It presents a spiritual context of the connection between the spirits of Ramatis, Rochester and Allan Kardec over the last 2,500 years, revealing the background of Spiritism, Allan Kardec's choice for building it, and various revelations about panels involving the team of the Spirit of the Truth.

Cosmic Reminder. It presents the message that Jesus left us in his five main teachings, and facts never before revealed by John the Evangelist in the first century of the Christian era.

The Master's Smile. The spirits of an uncle of Jesus, Cleopas and his father, Joseph, relate unknown facts of the life of Jesus: his travels as a young man and how the choice of the apostles occurred, revealing his greatest mark of love: the smile.

The Testament of Jesus. New approach to the beatitudes announced by Jesus in the Sermon on the Mount, revealing panels of his will for mankind.

In the Heavens of Greece. Dialogue between the Greek philosophers Socrates, Plato and Aristotle updating teachings of the past and addressing topics such as planetary and cosmic citizenship, universalism and contemporary political practices.

Behind the Scenes of Light I and II. Messages received at the meetings of the Atlan Study Group that embroider themes such as: (volume 1) karmic mechanisms, functioning of the human psyche, self improvement and inner reformation, planetary transition, spiritual genetics and the sidereal exiles; (volume 2) the Atlantean empire, consequences of suicide, Jesus and Sai Baba, UFOs, parallel lives, astral and spiritual cities, white fraternity and the origin of man, among others.

BOOKS PUBLISHED BETWEEN 2001 AND 2006

Extraterrestrial and extraphysical beings, as well as spiritual mentors, were the intelligences behind the following books that can be read separately because they have particular contexts:

Jesus and the Enigma of the Transfiguration. The real meaning of the transfiguration of Jesus and the facts of the final period of his life, brought by the narrative of James, Elijah and Moses.

Extraterrestrial Factor. It presents evidence of various extraterrestrial factors as the only possible explanation for many events that have occurred since the beginning of time and that are still considered legends. There is an interview done by Jô Soares, a famous brazilian TV Talk show host, with Ellam about this book, available with english subtitles.

The Seventh Trumpet of the Apocalypse: The Return of Jesus. An unprecedented panorama of the Apocalypse of John explaining the origin and the reason of the Book of Revelation, the factors that led to Jesus being born on Earth, the second coming of Christ, and the meaning of the Last Judgment and the current planetary transition.

Jesus and the Druid of the Mountain. It narrates facts of the unknown youth of Jesus, his friendship with Joseph ofArimathea, and with his brother Thiago.

Chronicles of a New Time. Diverse reflections on past, present and future themes.

Poetic Inquisition. The book chronicles the post-death experience of the poet Yohan and leads to the perception of the differences and similarities between life on Earth and life in a different dimension of ours: the poets' heaven.

Web of Time. It narrates the coexistence of an apprentice with his professor of physics and the construction of a strong friendship, showing that it is greater than the time, the philosophies, the religions, the geographical borders and, mainly, the aspect of a spiritualistic being and the other A scientist. It was produced in conjunction with the astronomer José Renan de Medeiros.

BOOKS PUBLISHED SINCE 2010

From 2007 until 2010, Jan Val Ellam did not publish any books. It was a troubled moment in which he preferred to dedicate himself to his professional and personal activities. In 2010, according to him, he was kind of forced to publish again and the books started once more to be produced.

The Cosmic Drama of Yahweh. It reveals the history of the creation of this universe and its creator, marking the beginning of the chapters of the deep Cosmic Revelation.

The Spiritual Drama of Yahweh. It continues the presentation of the history of the creation and creator, now from the spiritual point of view, revealing the fall of the universal architect, the providences of the Superior Spirituality to help him solve the problem, the creation of man and its contribution in the creator's psyche.

The Earthly Drama of Yahweh. It presents the Eras of Universal Creation and how the repercussion of the process came to be established in the formation of our planetary nature, highlighting the enigmatic gaps in it what remains to this day without convincing scientific explanations.

Divine Favor. Why was earthly life generated? What is its function? What lies behind the training that the human being suffered to worship a creator-god? Should we worship some transcendent entity? Who?

The time has come for us, even with hesitant steps, to uncover the aspects of truth that are under veils imposed on us by unknown facts.

After all, are there divine favors? What if everything is contrary to what we were accustomed to think?

Letters to Yahweh. Questions and remarks from enlightened human beings about the problem of universal problematic creation would like to address to the creator and that, surprisingly, he himself decided to respond.

At the request of the recipient, the letters produced by Mônica Camargo, after reading the three books that compose "the cosmic, spiritual and earthly dramas of Yahweh", were answered and transformed in this book.

The Big Data of the Creator. Imagine a creator who decides to work out a game in which the effective control of the parts allows the domination of the whole, and why each part needs to be monitored with no margin for surprises.

Despite the pre-established script, pieces particularized, acquired distinct personalities, free of any automatic judgment, and only the creator has the option to reconquer these individuals through a religious supercontrol, established in fear, to see if it would still be possible to control them.

This is the mental-operational background of the game that happens behind the kind of life we have on Earth and we are not even aware of it.

The Creator's Big Data reveals what was previously hidden in the "book of life," referenced in the Apocalypse. It's adult reading!

Memories of Yahweh. Records of the attempts of joint reflection proposed by the biblical creator, always in the sense of reaffirming his attempt to convince about the fulfillment of his designs for terrestrial creatures.

Philosophical Inquisition. An uncommon account of encounters in a parallel environment, involving the creator at first, and then adding the participation of the other members of the Trimurti, in dealing with instigating themes around the pretended domain that beings considered as mythological, always exercised on the humanity - a simple but crucial biological experience - until it has escaped the control of its creators.

Trimurtian Inquisition - Time of Apostasy (bets). Narrative of an unthinkable debate between the Lords of the Trimurti - Brahma, Vishnu and Shiva - around the bankruptcy of the policy they have practiced since the beginning of the times of universal creation, which end points to the most singular occurrence already happening among living beings, in this parallel environment, from which they seek to follow everything that has happened and is happening in our biological universe.

The Electrons rebellion - Among the fundamental particles of matter, pointed out by physics, the electrons have an unusual and little known characteristic: to host, in their "intimacy", the information produced since the "zero moment" of their history - which began a few seconds after "Big Bang" - until the present times, and so it will be as long as the universe does not end its existence.

The psyche of the various species (the strongest, the predators) of the universal nature that were born programmed to liquidate other forms of life and thus, through imperative violence, maintain the "survival of the strongest" as the tonic of inclement living , have soiled the "inner existence" of these agents of cosmic information.

Electrons seem to have no logical proposition - at least for the time being - to question why things are like this, but, strangely enough, there is still evidence and evidence that some premise in them no longer supports accumulating marks of suffering and other categories that embellish and criminalize existence.

This theme was never addressed in the canons of human culture, but due to "urgencies and needs" yet unknown to planetary logic, it has now become imperative to address it. It's a reading for grownups!

The Smile of Pandora. The story of a being who, in its origin, was nothing of human, and who came to a new kind of life due to an intrigue between Zeus and Prometheus.

This is a story that was lost in the mists of a strange and perverse past, which is now revealed to its descendants.

The book is about her life, which happened in immemorial time, and her legacy of "demon made woman". She is the progenitor of a rational humanity and her history is now available by the very voice of her strange personality.

The Guardian of Eden. What is still fiction for many, in this book, a being who is an example of an Autonomous Artificial Intelligence, relates pages of the Biblical past for having been circumstantial witness of some of those events.

An angel-clone of the hierarchy, he was ordered by the universal creator to remain as a planetary guardian for many millennia, which led him to become attached to the species whose historical process he observed, according to the order received, which forced him to closely follow the episodes since the days of the Garden of Eden.

He saw Jesus being crucified as he perceived the strife between the creator and the one who was respected among all in the hierarchy, and who had become human just to fulfill what was established between them.

He observed the facts, but never valued them with the standard of our logic, because his nature, which marks his psyche, is absolutely different from that which characterizes human nature.

Nowadays, having absorbed a little of the "earthly way," he strives to send messages that he must at all moments send to those who compose the hierarchy around the creator.

Like all others, he awaits the outcome of the "trimurtian disputes" which will define - what is already in the process of being defined - the terms of Jesus promised return and the reintegration of Earth to cosmic coexistence.

Atlantis Earth – The signal of Land's End. The first book of a trilogy that rescues the forgotten pages of the Lucifer Rebellion, as well as its relationship with the figure of Sophia, the Cosmic Christ, who later became a man under the personality of Jesus.

It tells of the arrival of rebels on the planet, known in the traditions of the past as fallen angels, and the interactions of these beings with the plot that was already unfolding on Earth, in those days when the rational human being was about to emerge.

These were the times of the formation of what would become

the future Atlantean empire, which remained shrouded in mystery, is now beginning to be revealed. In these days several extraterrestrial and extraphysical beings were present on Earth.

Atlantis Earth – The north fleet. The Capelin Bio-Demo Saga - including the headquarters of the Lucifer rebellion - now based on Earth in alternative realities underlying the planet, reaches dramatic moments without Sophia signaling any support.

The rebels, grouped in Benem, are part of a task force that, for millennia, was denominated as the North Fleet, around the ship "Espheron".

In addition to the "Beings of the Portals" (the so-called "Gods of Greek Mythology"), humans come to live with a "Conglomerate of Realities" coupled with the planet.

The decay began to mark all the established forces at the same time that the humans began to turn into the possible heirs of Earth.

As everyone weakened, the one who would later be known as Satan retained his strength, since the "Age of his dominion" was yet to begin.

Atlantis Earth – The human age. Due to various cataclysms, the "Atlantean culture and its many bases" came to an end, as did the weakening of the various extraterrestrial and extraphysical forces that sought to dominate the planet, which led the human species to emerge as the most improbable heiress of the planet, as it ended up happening.

Len Mion (Satan) and Yel Luzbel (Lucifer) patrol the coming of the Messiah announced by the prophetic vein of the Hebrew people, while they persecute Jesus in the attempt to understand if he was the long-announced "conqueror".

The crucifixion occurs, the departure of Yel Luzbel from the surroundings around the planet, which causes Len Mion to take command of the rest of the rebellion, trying to disrupt, in any way, any interest that he saw to be of Sophia or of the "god of the Jews. "

Upon perceiving in Hitler a former companion of the bioemo condition, Len Mion dominates his mind and turns him into a puppet of his intention to build on Earth the last trench of the rebel movement to confront Sophia.

Homo Sapiens: From War to Sport. Is there a greater force behind the emergence of the "mother-molecule" in the distant terrestrial past, with the code of life already completely delineated - from which all living beings descend - or was it all a chance?

The fact is that "something" exists that guides the rhythm of evolution, between accidents and incidents, in this or that direction, as if taking the newest product of planetary nature, our species homo sapiens, to a certain presumed model.

A merciless warrior one day, and later an athlete who vibrates in victory and accepts defeat without annihilating his opponent.

These are some of the reflections that are present in the instigating search for the understanding of what moves the human species along its painful and enigmatic evolutionary road.

These books are for those who seek to understand possible aspects around a "truth" that for a long time remained hidden.

Human romanticism was led to think that finding panels of truth would necessarily be synonymous with rejoicing, of satisfaction and spiritual comfort, when it is not so.

Maybe that's why in Shiva Samhita it was stated that "the anguish was present throughout the universe," and that in the Gospel of Thomas Jesus enigmatically said that, "he who seeks the truth, should never stop seeking; however, in finding it, he will be disturbed, only later to equilibrate and be able, then, to be sovereign over the process of life. "

My homage to those who never stopped seeking.

Jan Val Ellam

9 788562 411519